What Christian Leaders Are Saying About This Book

Unbelievers do not speak Christianese. Speaking Christianese to an unbeliever is like speaking Swahili to a German. This book shows Christians how to speak lovingly and relationally to the world around us.

Dr. Tony Evans
Founder, The Urban Alternative
Senior Pastor, Oak Cliff Bible Fellowship, Dallas, Texas

In *Learning the Language of Babylon*, Terry Crist reveals a brilliant strategy for invading the kingdoms of this world. One cannot read this book without being challenged. Hope for the future is clearly outlined in every chapter. Read with care.

Bishop Earl Paulk
Cathedral of the Holy Spirit, Atlanta, Georgia
Bishop, International Communion of Charismatic Churches

Terry Crist has written an excellent survey of why the Church must act now if she is to be consistent with her history and her mandate from God. Let Christ's victory on earth invade this planet, as "Joy to the World" declares, "far as the curse is found!" The book is theologically sound, well reasoned and eminently readable. I thoroughly enjoyed it and heartily recommend it.

Dennis Peacocke
President, Strategic Christian Services
and Fellowship of Christian Leaders

A map for the road back to becoming relevant as a Christian. *Learning the Language of Babylon* is not an option if we are to make disciples of all nations. Terry Crist is one of a new generation of revolutionaries sounding a clear trumpet preparing the Church for battle.

Rice Broocks
Senior Pastor, Bethel Chapel, Nashville, Tennessee
President, Morning Star International

Terry Crist has made a great contribution to twenty-first century Christendom by showing us the value and purpose of *Learning the Language of Babylon*. This is a vital truth that every Christian needs to learn. These principles will bless those called to be ministers in the marketplaces of the world. This book can be an important tool to help fulfill Christ's prayer for God's Kingdom to come and His will to be done on earth as it is in heaven.

Dr. Bill Hamon
Founder and President, Christian International
Bishop, Christian International Network of Churches

In *Learning the Language of Babylon*, Terry Crist boldly conveys the direction that the Holy Spirit has set for the Church. As a student of societal trends and culture, he warns the Christian not to retreat from the battle of ideas by closing off access to the marketplace. Terry skillfully teaches the reader how to understand and speak the language of Babylon—the postmodern culture in which we live—from a transformational perspective. This book is a survival guide for the twenty-first-century Christian and a must-read!

David Ireland
Senior Pastor, Christ Church, Montclair, New Jersey
Author, *Failure Is Written in Pencil*

Terry Crist has given definition in *Learning the Language of Babylon* to the growing isolation of the Church in relation to the world around us. If we are to fulfill Christ's mandate to disciple the nations, we must relate without compromise and communicate without being assimilated into the "Babylonian" culture. By the grace of God we can rise to this challenge.

John D. Williams, B.A., Th.B., M.Div.
Senior Pastor, River of Life Church, Deming, New Mexico

Terry Crist succinctly captures the heart of ministry in the twenty-first century—namely, the mandate to revive the Church and reclaim the culture. I recommend this book for anyone seeking to increase their effectiveness in serving the purpose of God in today's world.

Paul Daniel
Founder and Senior Pastor, His People Christian Ministries
Cape Town, South Africa

As any true ambassador endeavors to learn the language and culture of the people to whom he has been sent, so he may convey the will of his sovereign, so we must learn to communicate the Gospel to our world. Only when we learn the language of the culture can the heart of the Father be understood in our generation. Pastor Terry Crist has provided an invaluable aid to the Body of Christ by revealing great insight into the process of effectively ministering the word of reconciliation.

John & Mirjana Angelina
Founders, Gospel Life Center and Gospel Art Studio
Munich, Germany

Cutting-edge truth presented in a way that is biblically sound. You will be challenged by the prophetic urgency of these necessary principles of spiritual and cultural reformation. Terry Crist has presented this material in our nation and it has produced a necessary awakening among our leaders. Read this book carefully; there is change contained in every page.

Joao Cordoza
Founder and Senior Pastor, Abundant Life Churches
Lisbon, Portugal

This is an outstanding book of seminal importance. Terry Crist has accurately identified one of the most urgent needs of the Body of Christ at the dawn of the twenty-first century. Quite simply, it is the need for relevance. For too long the Church has opted out of society and withdrawn into the ghettos of inward-looking and self-serving Christian complacency. We have chosen to insulate ourselves from the world rather than actively engage with it and influence it for Christ and His Kingdom. *Learning the Language of Babylon* is a call to mature Christian nationhood.

Colin Dye
Senior Pastor, Kensington Temple
London, England

Terry Crist has always been a man ahead of his time. His insights and wisdom have influenced people for many years. Once again Terry comes through. This book is sure to take you to new levels in God.

Tim Storey
Founder, The Alternative, Hollywood, California

The prophetic anointing is not something to be treated casually. There is a compulsion, a fire in the bones. It captures our attention, compels us to face tough issues and leaves us with stark choices. In this urgently needed book, Terry Crist is a prophet on fire challenging the church to relevance without compromise, hope without hysteria and a future without futility, in clear bold tones.

Andrew J. Shearman
President, Reformation International Ministries

Good News! *Learning the Language of Babylon* is evidence that there is a new breed of Christians arising who understands not only the power of the Holy Spirit, but the purpose for the power. In the tradition of the great Protestant reformers and with the spirit of a modern Charismatic, Terry Crist sends a wake-up call to the entire body of Christ: it's time to embrace our mandate to disciple nations, transform cultures and build civilizations to the glory of God.

Joe Dunlap
Pastor, New Covenant Fellowship
Sublette, Kansas

Other Books by the Author

The Image Maker
The History Shaper
Interceding Against the Powers of Darkness

learning the
LANGUAGE OF BABYLON

CHANGING THE WORLD
BY ENGAGING THE CULTURE

TERRY M. CRIST

Chosen Books

A Division of Baker Book House Co
Grand Rapids, Michigan 49516

Published by Chosen Books
A division of Baker Book House Publishing Company
P.O. Box 6287
Grand Rapids, MI 49516-6287

Printed in the United States of America

Library of Congress Cataloging-in-Publication Data

Crist, Terry M., 1965–
    Learning the language of Babylon : changing the world by engaging the culture / Terry M. Crist.
       p.   cm.
    Includes bibliographical references and index.
    ISBN 0-8007-9287-4 (cloth)
    ISBN 0-8007-9288-2 (pbk.)
    1. Evangelistic work—United States. 2. Christianity and culture—United States.
I. Title.
BV3793.C68   2001
261'.0973—dc21   00-065841

For current information about all releases from Baker Book House, visit our web site:
http://www.bakerbooks.com

CONTENTS

This book is dedicated to my firstborn son,
Terry Michael III,
who carries not only my name
but also my passion for generational transformation.
May you never lose sight of your mission in Babylon.

ACKNOWLEDGMENTS

Billy Graham's first ministry slogan was "Geared to the Times. Anchored to the Rock." That motto is just as relevant now as it was then. *Learning the Language of Babylon* is my attempt to inspire the Church to societal infiltration without compromising the principles of righteous living. I am indebted to a number of people who have succeeded in the challenge of "gearing and grounding" me during the process of writing this book.

First, I want to express my deepest appreciation to my wife, Judith, for encouraging me to allow my reach to exceed my grasp. Through her continual motivation I am preaching and reaching for the emergence of a new generation of reformers.

Special thanks to David Ireland for inspiring the development of this concept, and to Walter Walker for encouraging me to merge the theological with the inspirational. I have seen new vistas through your respective ministries and have set sail in search of them.

Without the assistance of Bridget Jentzsch, Sonja Brown and Jill Williams, this book would still be somewhere between my cluttered memory bank and my exhausted word processor. Thank you for co-laboring in the design and development of this work.

Finally my heart is continually overwhelmed by the love and affirmation of a courageous church-planting team who left the comfort zone in order to relocate to Scottsdale, Arizona. Together we are learning the language of our community, and by the grace of God we will effect spiritual and cultural change. Let the reformation begin!

1

LIVING BEHIND ENEMY LINES

It was the scorching summer of 605 B.C. The
air was pungent with the stench of dried sweat and blood. Chained
together, four young men stumbled along the dusty trail that led to
Babylon. Physically exhausted and emotionally depleted, their
heads hung in humiliation. The silence was broken by an occasional muffled sob as the gravity of their loss sank deeper into their
consciousness. Tormented by unanswered questions, they had to
summon everything within them just to refrain from screaming
aloud, "Jehovah, where were You when we needed You most?"

Why had God allowed Jerusalem to be overthrown? To add to the devastation of their defeat, they knew this was not the first time God's chosen people had been conquered by the ruling powers of a heathen nation.

In the tenth century before Christ, the children of Israel had been divided into two separate nations. The smaller of the two was Judah, consisting of the tribes of Judah and Benjamin. The remaining ten tribes made up the nation of Israel. Each sinned by disregarding God's law and turning a deaf ear to His prophets.

In 722 B.C. the king of Assyria arrayed his armies against the tribes of Israel and conquered them. Whenever the Assyrians defeated a nation, they scattered the conquered citizenry among other nations under their control. The Assyrians believed that taking the survivors captive into foreign lands would obliterate their identity as a nation and prevent them from rising up and fighting for their independence. That was the way the Assyrians dealt with the nation of Israel. After defeating and dispersing it in this manner, Israel was never heard of again. Even today it is referred to as the "lost tribes of Israel."

Three generations later, following the same brutal pattern of destruction, King Nebuchadnezzar of Babylon returned with a vengeance. In typical fashion, the Jews retreated into Jerusalem, abandoning the countryside in the process.

Jerusalem, built high on a hill, was an impenetrable fortress— or so its inhabitants thought. Its elevation enabled it to bask in the glow of the afternoon sun, giving it the appearance of a golden city. The ancient world saw Jerusalem as the place where heaven and earth met. Equipped with interior wells and previously stored provisions, Jerusalem's citizens settled in for a long, arduous battle, determined to defy their enemies, no matter how long it took. The standoff lasted almost two years. Eventually Judah was defeated and subjugated. In the violent battle that preceded her downfall, villages were destroyed, homes burned and survivors taken into captivity.

Even more devastating than any personal loss was the invasion of Solomon's Temple. The Jews believed that this sacred site was the earthly sanctuary of Jehovah—His dwelling place, His material home. Yet the Babylonian barbarians defiled the Temple, stripping it and setting fire to the space where the Ark of the Covenant once rested. Many of the priests were slain in the sanctuary, and the sacred vessels carried away to be used in the worship of the Babylonian gods. Judah had been shamed and violated.

The remaining citizens of Judah and Jerusalem were quickly organized for the long march back to Babylon. It was the second and final deportation. None of those Jews would ever again see their homeland or worship in their holy city. But the greatest battle was yet to come. Within days they would be thrown into a culture that ridiculed their faith and oppressed their worship.

Everything the Jews loved and valued became a faint memory. Jerusalem was destroyed, the Temple reduced to rubble and the remaining priesthood scattered to the four winds. The customs that had given meaning to them as God's chosen people were lost. The Psalms reveal the torment they felt when their captors mocked them and urged them to sing one of the songs of Zion. "How shall we sing the LORD's song in a foreign land?" they lamented (Psalm 137:4). They were the people of God in exile.

Babylon the Battleground

The battle between Judah and Babylon is a physical picture of the spiritual battle that has raged since the beginning of time. In both the Old and New Testaments, Babylon and Jerusalem are identified as the earthly representations of the epic struggle between the forces of righteousness and unrighteousness. These two cities symbolize opposing ways of relating to God and all of life.

Babylon represents man in his lowest estate separated from God and alienated from his original purpose. The very word *Babylon* means "to confuse, disintegrate, fragment and disunite." We do not have to look hard to see the evidence of this moral and spiritual fragmentation everywhere around us—the obvious influence of demonic spirits at work in the kingdoms of this world. Seeking to abort the potential of every single person alive today, the spirit of Babylon has infiltrated many aspects of contemporary Christianity through false doctrine and immoral living. The apostle John describes Babylon as "the great harlot . . . with whom the kings of the earth committed fornication, and the inhabitants of the earth were made drunk with the wine of her fornication" (Revelation 17:1–2).

The spirit of Babylon is expressed in our day through liberal theology and spiritual tolerance, producing religious syncretism, a mixture of the holy and the profane. The clearest expression of the spirit of Babylon in contemporary culture is found, I believe, in the philosophy of moral relativism. Make no mistake; moral relativism has roots in distorted theology. Espousing the values of spiritual tolerance, truth is bartered away in the name of inoffensive Christianity. Professing a form of godliness, moral relativism denies the power inherent in the pure Gospel—the very power needed to break the stranglehold of relativism over our generation.

There is no doubt that American culture has changed dramatically over the past century from a biblical basis to one that is, at best, religiously pluralistic, and in many areas blatantly anti-Christian. What has happened in Europe is even more dramatic. Some missionary organizations have reclassified Great Britain, the greatest missionary-sending nation in history, as a pagan or unevangelized nation. As Dorothy once said to Toto, "I don't think we're in Kansas anymore."

The reference point of our American cultural decline is usually considered to be somewhere in the middle of the twentieth century. That does not mean the Church as a whole was more spiritually minded, more passionate for Christ or more dedicated to His service fifty years ago. That was simply the time when our withdrawal from the culture became obvious for the entire world to see. While we were looking the other way, the world changed and we were unprepared for it. The question remains, however: *How did we go from being the social majority to being cultural captives in three generations? And why did it happen?*

An old Chinese proverb says, "If you want to know what water is, don't ask the fish." Never having seen any other kind of environment, a fish lacks the ability to judge its own surroundings. It cannot conceptualize life in another form or setting; it has no knowledge of the alternative. In like fashion, most citizens of contemporary Western culture have become so immersed in our way of life that we have overlooked the biblical response to it. Our proximity to the progressive secularization of society has clouded our ability to discern the nature and cause of our captivity.

It is difficult, in other words, for us to properly appraise the nature of our own cultural crisis. We tend to begin our evaluation with certain presuppositions that eventually lead to the conclusions we had hoped to discover in the first place.

The alternative, however, is far more dangerous. We must not hide our heads in the sand, hoping the cultural crisis will go away. Until we face our weakness, we will never have the grace to spiritually displace it. At some point our generation must be willing to reject the confining limitations of our own cultural perspective and review our position from a biblical worldview.

Because the harsh reality is, the Western world has abandoned its moral compass. We have traded our collective conscience, our sense of right and wrong, for freedom from restraint. Prior to our recent cultural shift toward postmodernism, most individuals, before making any decision that would affect their lives, asked themselves, *Is this the right thing to do?* We were accustomed to considering the long-term consequences of our personal actions. But that was at a time in our history when we used biblical standards rather than emotions to govern our choices. Professor Allan Bloom laments:

> There is one thing a professor can be absolutely certain of: Almost every student entering the university believes, or says he believes, that truth is relative. Relativism is necessary to openness; and this is the virtue, the only virtue, which all primary education for more than fifty years has dedicated itself to inculcating.[1]

Babylonian philosophy pervades every facet of society, from the White House to the schoolhouse. It even makes an occasional appearance at the church house. This subtle, deceptive spirit seeks to enslave entire nations by seducing and manipulating the minds of men and women away from the Jerusalem pattern for living. And when the head is sick, so is the body (see Isaiah 1:5–6).

In stark contrast, Jerusalem represents the reality of the spiritual promise of life in the Kingdom of God. This promise was partially fulfilled in the natural city that once towered above the nations as the dwelling place of God (see Deuteronomy 12:11). The Jewish people were convinced that Jerusalem's history as a free city was neither accidental nor the result of its natural defenses alone. This beloved city, they believed, was the recipient of nothing less than divine favor. To the natural Jew, Jerusalem represented everything sacred in society.

But the greater expression of life in the Kingdom will be revealed in full measure when the New Jerusalem rises out of the ashes of the old. In the New Testament context, all believers are citizens of this heavenly city. Paul the apostle describes it like this:

> It is written that Abraham had two sons: the one by a bondwoman, the other by a freewoman. But he who was of the bondwoman was born according to the flesh, and he of the freewoman through promise, which things are symbolic. For these are the two covenants: the one from Mount Sinai which gives birth to bondage, which is Hagar—for this Hagar is Mount Sinai in Arabia, and corresponds to Jerusalem which now is, and is in bondage with her children— but the Jerusalem above is free, which is the mother of us all.
>
> Galatians 4:22–26

The Jerusalem-Babylon battle continues to be expressed in every nation in every generation. It is a spiritual battle transcending time, space, geography and race. Like the prisoners of Nebuchadnezzar in the summer of their shame, we are engaged in a conflict to preserve the remnants of righteousness in our society while also taking back the ground lost in previous conflicts.

Where Are the Freeborn?

Unlike the four Israelites at the beginning of this chapter, my generation was born in exile. This confinement was not defined as precisely as the captivity of Daniel and his friends in Babylon. The battle lines were blurred, the face of the enemy obscured and our objective not clearly identified. Like you, I was born into *cultural* captivity.

Toward the end of the nineteenth century, the Church in America was faced with combating three ideas that were quickly gain-ing popularity: scientific materialism, higher biblical criticism and a renewal of seventeenth-century rationalism. A "modern" worldview was emerging in place of the biblical synthesis that had been prevalent in Western culture. Postmodernism was soon to follow. These forces laid siege to the North American Church, just as surely as Nebuchadnezzar surrounded Jerusalem to destroy it. Sydney Alstrum, perhaps the foremost authority on the history of religion in America, described this battlefield as "the most fundamental controversy to wrack the churches since the Reformation."[2] As a result of the controversy that followed, the evangelical Church was divided.

On the one hand, there were those who capitulated rather than engage in a battle of ideas. In other words, they made peace with the enemies of the Kingdom by surrendering orthodox beliefs such as biblical creationism, human sin, the virgin birth of Christ and the inerrancy of Scripture. Although the liberal faction of the Church forsook many of the essential doctrines of Christianity, they continued to embrace a form of the "dominion mandate."

Their vision for dominion without a commitment to biblical truth resulted in two forms of theology. The first came to be known as "the fatherhood of God and the brotherhood of man." Mankind was seen as basically good, while God was the all-loving Father whose tolerance of sin knew no end. This distorted theology discarded the concept of God as holy and righteous Judge. The second theological idea, the social gospel, was an effort not only to influence culture but to reform society, but it was reformation without the Word of God as the central focus.

The other major faction of the Church was made up primarily of those who were theologically conservative yet out of touch with the cultural crisis. My spiritual forebears fell into this camp. They remained faithful to the Word of God and the fundamentals of the faith (hence the term *fundamentalists*). But although they did not capitulate to their doctrinal enemies, they did not exactly run to the battle either. In a way they surrendered the holy city and lined up for the trip to Babylon. In my estimation they abandoned all hope of cultural influence and began preparing instead for Armageddon. Most of them were, or soon became, radical premillennial dispensationalists. Because of human depravity and the overwhelming presence of evil in the world, they expected that the rule of Christ over the nations could be expressed only in the Millennium.

Not all adherents of this view of eschatology have expressed such an escapist mentality. In many cases, however, it offered a good excuse to abandon a world that had suddenly turned on them.

Members of this faction of the Church were, for the most part, less educated and from a lower socioeconomic segment of society. Rather than engage in the battle of ideas, they retreated from the mainstream of culture into the holy huddle. This began to transform them from a dominant intellectual and cultural influence in the world to a minority sect. Some fundamentalist extremists even adopted a theology of anti-intellectualism. Their response to the scientific biases of the nineteenth century was to divorce Christianity from reason and history. They contended that the discoveries of science make no difference because faith and truth are unconnected. This was a tragic mistake and a fundamental misunderstanding of the foundation of Christianity. What is unique about the Christian faith is that it is *rooted* in reason and history!

Thus the United States of America, like Judah in the summer of 605 B.C., encountered Nebuchadnezzar. The battle lines were clearly drawn. Two hundred fifty years of Christian influence were not reversed overnight. But most social institutions, like civil government, universities, public schools and the media, which were once dominated by Christian thinking, were reshaped by a secular mindset. Reminiscent of Daniel and his companions, the best and brightest of this generation began the long journey toward Babylon. Primarily through the media and the educational system, young leaders began training for service in the secular courts of world systems. And like those princes of Judah, they could hardly help but wonder, *How can we sing the Lord's song in a strange land?*

Noted historian Arnold Toynbee once studied 21 civilizations and discovered five characteristics common to disintegrating societies, ranging from Rome to China, from the Aztecs to ancient Babylon. Very few "advanced" civilizations were simply overrun by other nations; most were destroyed by internal culture wars. Every society he examined shared in a common crisis. They seemed to lack a sense of stability, believing that life was meaningless and out of control. As a result they succumbed to escapism or social negligence, retreating into entertainment and recreation. Tolerance rendered them powerless to transform the social decline. Yielding to their unrestrained appetites, they abandoned moral absolutes and embraced wholesale promiscuity. And these disintegrating societies contended with a continual sense of guilt and self-hatred.[3]

Sir Arnold Toynbee's description fits both ancient Babylon and modern America. The Babylonian influence on Western culture has precipitated a fundamental shift in the way we now live our lives.

The battle for the nations of the earth, I am convinced, will ultimately be a struggle for control of the culture—who is in charge and who will set the social agenda. As James Dobson and Gary Bauer wrote, "Nothing short of a great civil war of values rages throughout North America. Two sides with vastly differing and incompatible worldviews are locked in bitter conflict that permeates every level of society; it is a war over ideas."[4] The definitive question facing the Church of the twenty-first century is this: *Who is in charge?*

Held Captive by Our Theology

America has been invaded not by a foreign military but by powerful demonic forces that enslave the mind and spirit. Derek Prince once commented that the demons that have invaded America are "sophisticated." It is not that Africa or India suffers under a greater demonic influence than we do in America. It is simply that our demons are "refined." Rather than being readily identifiable, they are hiding in the present culture of the day. The principalities and powers I am describing are those spiritual forces that have targeted the current generation. Their aim is to invade, enslave and employ the cream of our youth in the kingdom of darkness.

Like many evangelicals, I was raised believing that redemption was limited to a few determined Christians who resisted all forms of worldliness and remained free from spiritual defilement until the end of the age. The last days, we were convinced, would be precipitated by a great falling away, and a pure remnant of enduring Christians would barely resist the overwhelming spirit of deception that was being released to test the Church. Our greatest hope was to be evacuated miraculously from this God-forsaken world just hours before the powers of darkness closed in for the final strike.

We acknowledged, ironically, that Jesus' death on the cross was the greatest act in all of human history. We saw it as the triumph of life conquering death, the Son of God removing the curse from the sons of men. But even though we attested to the defeat of principalities and powers at the cross, our primary goal in life (and this was true through much of the twentieth century) was to be rescued from this demonized generation. We had developed a remnant theology to insulate us from our pain.

In our theological confusion we harbored a hidden hope that the Gospel would ultimately be victorious, while personally lacking the faith to believe that anything positive could happen on this darkened planet. It was as if our systematic theology was at odds with the prophetic hope that lay within us. Tragically, in our spiritual and theological insecurity, we allowed God to be marginalized in His very own world.

As the Church retreated from the public arena, the spirit of Babylon gained a foothold in contemporary culture and began to secularize our nation, making righteous principles less meaningful and religious institutions more ghetto-ized. The enemy was allowed to push everything righteous in our culture over to the sidelines, making Christianity a fringe element, a subculture within the greater culture. We allowed everything that defined us as a God-fearing people to be undermined or removed. The values we once held dear slowly disintegrated before our eyes.

As the culture deteriorated, we Christians focused our attention on other things, inward things, those things that escapists always focus on when the pain of captivity becomes greater than the hope for change. We stopped planning for the future and began focusing on our escape. Rapture ferver swept through the Church like a raging fever trying to burn out the infection of our disappointment. Slowly our theology began to shift from the dominion mandate; our songs started focusing on our departure, and a new "situational eschatology" emerged in its place. The desire to reform society was replaced by the longing to escape the pain of watching our culture worsen. We slowly began to accept our exile as permanent.

An Unlikely Proponent

As the son of a pastor, I loved to hear the thrilling stories of Daniel's mighty exploits of faith. I never tired of hearing of his refusal to eat the king's meat, his faith while in the lions' den and his ability to interpret the handwriting on the wall. *But I never saw his life as an example of how to reclaim the cultural terrain from the hand of the enemy!* My Christian subculture had insulated me from the need to relate successfully to contemporary society.

Daniel was not slow to respond to the challenge, as we were. In fact, his understanding seems to have developed quickly after the Babylonians took him captive. Somehow this remarkable young man (the Hebrew text intimates that he and his fellow prisoners were *naharim,* or teenagers) sorted out the challenge of demonstrating his faith in a hostile culture. He was willing to learn the *language* of Babylon without being nourished by the *spirit* of Babylon. And in so doing, he established a pattern for each of us attempting to serve as missionaries to a "foreign" culture. We will never transform contemporary society if we are unwilling to learn its language. We must sing our song in the land of Babylon.

When a Japanese manufacturer was asked recently by his North American counterpart, "What is the best language in which to learn to do business?" the man responded, "My customer's language."[5] Likewise we must learn to speak the language of the culture in which we have become exiled—and this necessitates a measure of vulnerability on our part. Without becoming willing to acknowledge our present captivity, learn from our past mistakes and reorient ourselves toward the future, we will never have the transforming effect on culture that God wants us to have.

Acknowledging our identity as believers in exile forces us to reexamine the process that led to our captivity in the first place. Following the fall of Jerusalem, those who were held captive in Babylon were forced to reevaluate everything they considered sacred. That process led to the strengthening of certain practices and the rejection of other powerless traditions. Likewise, if we are to return from exile, we must be willing to sift through what we have been taught, strengthening timeless truths while rejecting traditions that have no application in our generation. Those Jewish exiles would never return to the good old days in Jerusalem. Neither will we as believers in the twenty-first century. We have two options before us: to surrender the battle and sacrifice unborn generations on the altar of our apathy, or to reengage the culture from a different vantage point, armed with a new strategy.

The only way back to cultural and spiritual Jerusalem is by a different path than the one on which we walked into exile. We will never recover the former glory by retracing the return path to Jerusalem. Times have changed and the good old days are gone forever. We must chart a new course.

This book is an attempt to reevaluate certain spiritual and theological positions that have led, in part, to our current exile. I will not attempt to offer a comprehensive diagnosis or the final prescription. I simply offer a panoramic assessment of the current crisis and the beginning point for the long journey home.

And I feel compelled to state at the outset that I am not writing as one who has perfected the art of societal infiltration. My credentials suggest that no one is a more unlikely candidate than I am! Yet having seen the need, I cannot ignore the mission. I am on a journey—a mission to rescue the lost and reclaim the culture.

2

THE FRAMEWORK OF CAPTIVITY

> The West appears to have said its definitive
> farewell to a Christian culture. . . . Our secular
> colleagues are happy to recognize the debt our
> civilization owes to the Christian faith to the
> extent that the faith, having been absorbed by cul-
> ture itself, has become simply another cultural
> artifact. Christianity has become a historical fac-
> tor subservient to a secular culture rather than
> functioning as the creative power it once was.[1]
>
> Yale professor Louis Dupré

Nebuchadnezzar was no amateur when it
came to conquering nations. He was the first ruler in history to
dominate the entire known world. After confiscating the sacred fur-
nishings from the Temple in Jerusalem, the king carted them back
to Babylon and placed them in the temple of Bel, one of that nation's
chief deities. This single act of defiance gives us insight into his

diabolical intention to eradicate every vestige of "native religion"—and therefore righteousness before the one true God—in the lives of his captives.

Thousands of young Jews were marched off to Babylon to be assimilated into the courts of civil service. Many of the captives died during the harsh trip. They did not travel directly east from Jerusalem to Babylon, because the journey would have been impossible across the burning sand of the Arabian Desert. Instead they headed north along the Fertile Crescent, then south along the Euphrates River. It was the same route, ironically, that Abraham had taken to the Promised Land thirteen hundred years earlier. Now Daniel was being taken as a captive back to the land of his forefathers.

Since it was not productive to kill everyone, King Nebuchadnezzar developed a program designed to disenculturate the Jews—that is, to strip them of the elements that gave them their identity as a distinct people group. He isolated the young men who were in good health, intelligent and handsome, from the rest of the captives, and attempted to demoralize them. Everything they had ever known and loved was stripped away as they were introduced to a civilization filled with peculiar sights, smells and sounds. It would be safe to say that most did not arrive with a vision to transform their pagan environment. Rather they settled in and tried to make the best of a bad situation.

Notice several similarities between the challenge facing Daniel and our present spiritual condition.

First, Daniel was a righteous young man sent to live in an oppressive, ungodly environment at a time when God seemed to have withdrawn His blessing from Judah. Daniel's position was much like that of believers today. Ours is not a pagan society; it is a post-Christian one. Paganism is a pre-Christian condition, the atmosphere that exists before the Gospel is proclaimed and demonstrated in a culture. A post-Christian society develops when the Gospel is rejected, leaving the people to wallow in pride and self-sufficiency.

Second, Daniel was under tremendous pressure to conform to the societal expectations held by his captors. Although he was free to practice his religion privately, he was required to respond in a "politically correct" manner when in the presence of the Babylonians. He was expected to eat their meat, honor their dignitaries, even listen to their music. But in spite of their demands, he did only what his conscience allowed him to do, standing firm in the face of temptations, testings and trials.

Third, Daniel fought hard to escape the attempts of the Babylonians to define, label and reject his true identity. This was the greatest battle of all. After the young men of Judah were taken into captivity, the first act of Ashpenaz, prince of the eunuchs, was to change their names. "He gave Daniel the name Belteshazzar; to Hananiah, Shadrach; to Mishael, Meshach; and to Azariah, Abed-Nego" (Daniel 1:7).

This practice has occasionally surfaced in modern times, too. In the late 1970s, for example, the war-torn country of Albania adopted the practice of the Babylonians by requiring that the names of her citizens reflect the priorities and practices of that secular state. *Christianity Today* reported at the time that Albania "has joined the list of countries taking away one of the most personal and private possessions of its citizens: their names. . . . After all, someone named Abraham or Ruth or Mark might someday wonder where his name came from! And that could lead to a time-consuming search for a Bible or other religious literature. In the process, the unfortunately named Albanian might absorb some of the teachings of the outlawed book. That result, in the view of the government, would be very bad."[2]

What's in a Name?

Most people today name their children with little thought as to the spiritual overtones. In biblical times, however, the character and destiny of a child were thought to be revealed through his or her name. An infant was carefully guarded and observed for seven days after birth, during which time the parents had the responsibility of discovering and defining that child's destiny. On the eighth day following birth, every male Israeli child was circumcised and named. Imagine the incredible responsibility of observing your child for this short period of time in the hope of perceiving his character and destiny! Throughout the whole of his life, his name was the constant reminder of ancient history and future purpose.

Each of the four young men in captivity in Babylon carried Hebrew names reflecting a portion of the character and nature of almighty God. The name *Daniel* in Hebrew means "God's judge." Not only did Daniel judge the spiritual matters of his generation on behalf of Jehovah, but he also was a judge of the perverse culture of his day as he continued to live out the destiny encapsulated in his name. The name *Hananiah* means "beloved of the Lord." *Mishael* asks, "Who is like God?" And *Azariah* means "whom the Lord helps."

The Babylonians changed their names in order to transform their identities. With these new names they sought to erase the young Jewish men's pasts, to abort their destinies and to convince them to accept their captivity. Daniel's Babylonian name, *Belteshazzar,* means "Baal's prince." *Hananiah* was changed to *Shadrach,* which means "under the command of Aku, the moon god." *Mishael* was changed to *Meshach,* which asks not, "Who is like God?" but, "Who is like Aku?" And *Azariah* was changed to *Abednego,* which means "the servant of Nego," another of the Babylon deities.

But renaming these young princes of Judah accomplished nothing. Although Nebuchadnezzar possessed the ability to change their names, he remained powerless to transform their hearts. They knew who they were and why they were alive at that pivotal moment in Judah's history. The simple truth is, as long as *you* know who you really are, it does not matter what society calls you, or how much they ridicule you, or what label they place on you. It is only a matter of time before the real you arises and begins to disprove others' misconceptions.

As I wrote in *The Image Maker,* "Mistaken identity always results in a behavior out of accord with one's true identity. For the sake of illustration, let me describe it this way. If you can convince a man that he is a slave—when in fact he is a king by birth—then he will develop a slave mentality and will live far beneath his inherited right. In spite of who he is genetically, in spite of his heritability, he will never rise to the throne because he believed a lie concerning his identity."[3]

Whatever you allow to define your identity will have a corresponding effect on your sense of mission and purpose.

Amazingly, in spite of the vast store of information Christians have on the need to transform our culture, and the conviction that we must do this, we have done little to create any real change. The challenge for most people, I suspect, is not a lack of vision so much as it is a lack of understanding of our real identity as sons and daughters of God. The same is true of the world's need for holiness, discipleship and evangelism. If we Christians do not understand that we are salt and light in the present age, we will never succeed in transforming a generation.

The Measure of Grace, Personal and Cultural

Two significant themes, both of which run throughout the Scriptures, precede learning the language of Babylon. Neither is considered a cardinal doctrine, but both are vital to how we live our Christian lives each day. If you were to consider God's great plan of redemption the main plot of a drama acted out on the stage of history, these themes would be subplots.

The first is how the people of God are to respond when they find themselves in cultural or political captivity, faced with the pressures of intimidation, oppression or, in the extreme case, martyrdom. The second theme is cultural relevance—how the people of God relate to and interact in cultures that are unreceptive or even hostile to their faith.

Christians in many places around the world find themselves cultural captives in spiritual Babylon. But before we discuss the challenge of changing the culture, I want to examine the divine purpose behind captivity. How do we interpret the developments happening all around us? The answer has a lot to do with the way we relate to the culture as a whole and to individuals socially.

First, we know that the earth belongs to the Lord. He created it, upholds it and governs to the degree that sin is restrained from overcoming and destroying human civilization. In his landmark work *How Now Shall We Live?* former presidential aide Charles Colson writes:

Evangelism and cultural renewal are both divinely ordained duties. God exercises His sovereignty in two ways: through saving grace and common grace. We are all familiar with saving grace; it is the means by which God's power calls people who are dead in their trespasses and sins to new life in Christ. As God's servants, we at times may be agents of His saving grace, evangelizing and bringing people to Christ. But few of us really understand common grace, which is the means by which God's power sustains creation, holding back the sin and evil that result from the Fall and that would otherwise overwhelm His creation like a great flood. As agents of God's common grace, we are called to help sustain and renew His creation, to uphold the created institutions of family and society, to pursue science and scholarship, to create works of art and beauty, and to heal and help those suffering from the results of the Fall.[4]

Grace, when it is defined as unmerited favor, makes one think of the forgiveness of sin—that is, saving grace. But grace is also the divine enabling of God, as He helps us to do and be more than we ever could in our own strength. Grace is what elevates an individual or nation to greatness. The apostle Paul reveals the secret of his nation-shaking ministry in his letter to the Corinthians: "By the grace of God I am what I am, and His grace toward me was not in vain; but I labored more abundantly than they all, yet not I, but the grace of God which was with me" (1 Corinthians 15:10). Grace, to Paul, was not just forgiveness, but divine ability and virtue expressed by the Holy Spirit through believers. The grace of God enables a nation to be truly righteous, orderly, free and compassionate. Remove God's common or restraining grace, and that same nation descends into unbelief, immorality, violence and chaos.

You could think of the rise and fall of nations in terms of God's giving greater grace or removing His grace. Which brings us back to the question I just raised: How do we, as captives in Babylon, interpret the developments happening all around us?

Discerning the Purpose of Captivity

When a great enemy threatens the people of God, two competing interpretations ensue. The loudest voice usually comes from the "prophets of doom" crying out against the sins of the nation or the Church and warning of God's imminent judgment. Doomsayers often prophesy out of their own sense of cultural rejection. They feel disenfranchised by contemporary society, overwhelmed by the world around them and unable to do anything to change it. Consequently they have given up all hope, personally and theologically, for social and cultural redemption. They continue, in the tradition of Jonah, to prophesy doom and destruction out of unresolved conflicts in their own souls, even after the wrath of God has been abated. They cannot let go of the original message of judgment and destruction. Often they withhold mercy from others because they have never learned to receive mercy for their own personal weaknesses.

Not every pessimistic prediction of the future is motivated by a personal issue. It can be difficult, however, to sort out the word of the Lord from among a multitude of predictions introduced by Scripture verses or "Thus saith the Lord." I have learned that trying to bring a little balance to a dedicated prophet of doom is like trying to put out a fire by pouring fuel on it. The individual usually does not receive correction very well. And dismissal by society or correction by church leaders only serves to enflame the persecuted prophet.

There are always believers, on the other hand, who are as blindly optimistic as the doomsayers are pessimistic. Without weighing the issues carefully, they prophesy unconditional triumph in every challenge. Their prescription is to ignore the facts, believe the best and attempt to defeat the enemy without learning what brought about their captivity in the first place.

In his groundbreaking book *Roaring Lambs,* respected author and critical thinker Bob Briner writes:

> If the lambs will ever roar—if Christian faith is ever to gain acceptance in our culture—churches and Christian colleges must do a better job addressing the paucity of a Christian presence in American public life. The best way to start is to admit there's a problem. Set aside all those glowing church-growth statistics and acknowledge that Christian thought and values are almost completely absent in the mainstream of American culture. The only thing keeping us from such an admission is pride, and we all know what follows pride. So just admit it. We're not where we should be as people of God.[5]

How you respond to a crisis is always based on how you perceive the problem. The two most common interpretations of the reason behind our cultural decline are these:

1. It is the judgment of God brought upon us for our sins, so we must confess before Him; or
2. It is the devil coming in like a flood against the Kingdom and covenant people of God. Consequently we must rise up and take the land!

At certain times in the history of Israel, an approaching enemy had nothing to do with the Lord's judgment. It was simply an opportunity for God's people to trust Him to show Himself strong on their behalf. In those situations the proper response to impending destruction or captivity was to rise up in faith. Recall when Jehoshaphat sent out the singers praising God in front of the army. They stood still and saw the salvation of God (see 2 Chronicles 20:1–30). Or when Gideon gathered his little army to surround and defeat the Midianites, who had practically controlled Israel (see Judges 6–7). But at other times one of the two competing interpretations is clearly in view.

These two very different perspectives—"It must be God" and "It must be the devil"—were demonstrated in the first century when Titus and the Roman legions surrounded Jerusalem to lay waste to it. According to Josephus, the Jewish historian, many in Jerusalem expected the Almighty to send the Messiah (not Jesus of Nazareth, whom they had rejected) to save them from imminent destruction. Some even claimed to be the Messiah themselves.

But in light of Scripture, there is no question about what caused the destruction of Jerusalem in A.D. 70. Appearing before the Pharisees, Jesus pronounced a series of woes on them (see Matthew 23:13–36). He concluded by saying that, although they built tombs to the prophets, they were just like their fathers who killed them. Jesus was indicating that, once the religious leaders rejected the prophets and preachers, their cup of iniquity would overflow into judgment. What happened to Jerusalem, then, was the result of God's judgment.

The same principle of accumulated judgment is revealed in God's word to Abraham concerning the captivity of his descendants in

Egypt—judgment not toward the Hebrews but toward the Canaan-
ites. "Know for certain," God told him, "that your descendants will
be strangers in a country not their own, and they will be enslaved
and mistreated four hundred years. . . . In the fourth generation your
descendants will come back here, for the sin of the Amorites has
not yet reached its full measure" (Genesis 15:13, 16, NIV). The Genesis text suggests that the children of Israel remained as slaves in
Egypt until the Amorites had accumulated for themselves a suffi-
cient measure of judgment by which God would drive them out of
the Promised Land.

These same two factions—"It's the judgment of God" or "It's the
work of the enemy"—were also present in the seventh century B.C.
when Nebuchadnezzar destroyed Jerusalem and carted the Jews off
into captivity. Some thought it inconceivable that this abominable
pagan king was, in fact, raised up by God as a means of judgment
against Jerusalem. Years later, as a captive in Babylon, Daniel wrote,
"This decision is by the decree of the watchers, and the sentence by
the word of the holy ones, in order that the living may know that
the Most High rules in the kingdom of men, gives it to whomever
He will, and sets over it the lowest of men" (Daniel 4:17).

In the minds of certain Jews, Judah was not what she had been
spiritually, but she was certainly more righteous than the Babylonians. They should, therefore, rise up in faith because God was
their Deliverer. But others, including the prophet Jeremiah, understood that fighting was useless because they were facing the judgment of God—judgment that was long overdue. Because of the
increasing wickedness of the kings of Judah, God had determined
their punishment. For the sake of righteous men who sought the
Lord, judgment had been delayed for generations. But now God's
wrath had peaked and their fate was sealed.

Lessons from the University of Babylon

I am sure that after Nebuchadnezzar leveled the Temple, destroyed the city and carted off the contents to Babylon, there were
a lot of questions running through the minds of the survivors:

How could God let this happen? Has He forsaken us? Or was it God who orchestrated this whole thing in response to the sins of our nation? What is His purpose now that we find ourselves in captivity? How should we respond? And what on earth are we supposed to do now?

There were many more questions than answers on that long, dusty march to Babylon. As we examine our present cultural crisis in light of the captivity of Daniel, we must learn four fundamental lessons.

Lesson 1: Our Disposition Determines the Degree of Our Devastation

Judah had lost touch with her biblical moorings, her foundations of righteousness. Being filled with self-sufficiency and self-righteousness, her ears were plugged to the warnings of impending judgment and the prophetic exhortations to repent. She also looked down on her rival; defeated Israel must certainly have gotten what she deserved! By some standards, especially in the minds of those in Judah, the ten tribes constituting the nation of Israel were, by comparison, far more wicked.

Judah's false sense of security was predicated on her belief that God would protect His own Temple, if nothing else. And since that splendid Temple was in Jerusalem, surely God would not allow what had happened to Israel to come on her.

Not only did He allow it, but He raised up Nebuchadnezzar to do it! God was not as concerned about preserving external structures (as Judah found out) as He was about her attitude toward Him.

Attitude, as it relates to God's restraining grace, is clearly illustrated in Paul's letter to the Romans. He wrote that those who had puffed themselves up in their pride, and refused to acknowledge God, had been given over to their own foolish speculations. Then, three times, the apostle wrote that God "gave them up"—first to "the lusts of their hearts," then "to vile passions," and finally "to a debased mind" (Romans 1:24, 26, 28). Because of their pride and refusal to acknowledge God's truth that had been made evident to them, He removed the restraints and gave them over to their own sinful natures.

God did not have to make any special effort to send judgment on them. Without His restraining grace, they actually brought judgment on themselves by the desires and lust of their own hearts.

Sometimes nations increasing in unrighteousness are given over to the lust of their hearts, to depraved minds and to foolish speculations. Why? Because of their collective disposition. They honor themselves rather than God, and replace faith with foolish speculations.

But God's judgment is usually carried out with a redemptive purpose in mind. Throughout the seventy years of the Babylonian captivity, thousands of Jewish prisoners must have continued to ask, "Why were we overcome by the enemy, and what can we do to regain our freedom?" Captivity, whether to a foreign nation, a pagan culture or our own sin nature, is a humbling experience. The Jews were proud and self-sufficient no more. Regardless of whether we humble ourselves or are humbled by the finger of God, a changed attitude makes us candidates for a greater outpouring of His grace. As James wrote in his epistle, "He gives more grace. Therefore He says: 'God resists the proud, but gives grace to the humble'" (James 4:6).

The apostle Peter's instructions to young leaders could also be applied to nations: "Clothe yourselves with humility toward one another, because, 'God opposes the proud but gives grace to the humble.' Humble yourselves, therefore, under God's mighty hand, that he may lift you up in due time" (1 Peter 5:5–6, NIV).

Lesson 2: All Captivity Is Not Created Equal

The Babylonian captivity was very different than the bondage Israel had experienced in the land of Egypt. Her servitude under the hand of Pharaoh had been a brutal and emptying experience. Some of the great sites of Egypt were built with the slave labor of Jewish captives. Lacking property, dignity and human rights, the children of Israel adopted the diminished mentality of captivity.

Their suffering in Babylon, by contrast, was more subtle and sophisticated. For a people in subjection, the Jews in Babylon were granted a remarkable degree of liberty. They were allowed to own property, worship privately and pursue their own dreams, within certain boundaries.

After a journey of five hundred miles, the captives arrived in Babylon. As they entered the capital on Procession Street, they would have passed through the Ishtar gate and walked adjacent to Nebuchadnezzar's main palace, built in honor of the god Marduk. The roadway was paved with imported limestone and sometimes reached a width of 65 feet. This majestic entrance to the city was a double gate flanked with brightly decorated towers of blue-enameled brick.[6] The walls of the fortress were covered with geometric figures, engraved flowers and life-sized images of such animals as bulls, lions and dragons.[7]

Indeed, Babylon was the greatest civilized city in the world. Archaeologists tell us that its architecture was unmatched by any other metropolis in the known world. There were 43 temples in Babylon, including Nebuchadnezzar's personal house of worship. The streets of the city were lined with beautiful columns and pillars. The hanging gardens of Babylon are still known as one of the seven wonders of the ancient world. Great Babylonian libraries contained every book classified on every subject in the known world.

In the midst of this advanced culture, however, raged unbridled perversion, promiscuity and lack of moral restraint. It was a city intoxicated with its own power and filled with the very wealth it had taken from conquered cities throughout the world. It was in this atmosphere that the Jews were allowed certain freedoms and liberties.

Does it sound at all familiar? It is the same kind of captivity many Christians find themselves in today. In this subtle form of tyranny, hostages are expected not to push against the boundaries, not to challenge the status quo, but to be grateful for what they have. If Egyptian bondage could be compared to America's enslavement of Africans, then the Babylonian captivity might be paralleled by Jim Crow segregation—although we suffer nowhere near that level of degradation. The Church is allowed a great deal of freedom, but at the same time expected to stay in her place. So we find ourselves seated at the table of unilateral disarmament, saying to the enemy, "Just give us our tax-free status, leave us alone, and we will leave the popular culture to you."

Several years ago, in a time of intense soul-searching, the Lord asked me this startling question: *Who gave you the right to bargain off My property?* Though it was a simple question, it produced a major paradigm shift in my thinking. In a moment of revelation I felt I understood the purpose behind the question. Like many others, I had sat down at that table of unilateral disarmament with the enemy and said to him, in effect, "Don't bother us and we won't bother you! You can have the kingdoms of this world—entertainment, the arts, media, politics, athletics, law, economics—and we will take our Sunday school programs, Bible clubs, Christian conferences and home Bible studies. If you leave us alone, we'll leave you alone."

And we bargained off God's property! Because of our desire to escape the challenges of life, we have held a century-long fire sale, liquidating our interests and influence in all of popular culture.

This is the kind of captivity that negotiates a settlement and then calls it *freedom.* The Church as a whole, having felt the oppression and intimidation of the enemy at the gate, has negotiated a peace settlement rather than engage in the battle of ideas and cry out for a greater measure of God's restraining and preserving grace. A negotiated settlement is just another way of describing a modified surrender—whereas the nature of freedom is to break new ground and exceed the limits of what we have previously produced, known or accomplished. A negotiated settlement is the most dangerous form of captivity. It seduces you into believing that you are free when, in fact, you are a captive.

The same form of bondage progressively infiltrated the Laodicean church. They considered themselves self-sufficient; thought themselves rich when, in fact, they were wretched, poor, blind and naked. And this is the type of captivity from which the Western Church has yet to escape.

Lesson 3: Captivity Can Become the Catalyst for Change

Think about the remarkable character of Daniel, that extraordinary man who lived his life in pursuit of excellence in spite of stiff challenges. Early on in his captivity, Daniel came to recognize the fact that some things would never be as they once were.

One of the most difficult lessons in life is learning to deal with change that involves personal loss. Rick Warren once made this statement: "All growth is change. All change is loss. All loss is pain." Dozens of times while counseling people, I have heard them say, "Pastor, I just can't accept it. I just can't live with the way things are. Why did God let this happen? It isn't fair!" We seem to be more accepting of change when we feel empowered to determine the outcome of the events. But when circumstances are beyond our control, we feel anxiety. Faced with painful change, we often shut down emotionally. The result: arrested emotional and spiritual development.

The story is told of a little old man celebrating his hundredth birthday. A reporter interviewing him said, "I'll bet you've seen a lot of changes in your life."

The old man responded, "Yes, and I've been against every single one of them!"

Negative situations in our lives would not be so devastating if we began to view every form of change as an opportunity to move forward. When God brings change into your life, even when it catches you by surprise, it is still an opportunity to grow and to increase the quality of life God desires to give you. But this will happen only if you properly respond to the change.

Many present-day Christians never consider that God might be responsible for anything "negative" that happens in their lives. The Scripture does indeed say, "In all these things we are more than conquerors through Him who loved us" (Romans 8:37). But there is a connection many seem to miss between "all these things" and the trials referred to in the previous verse: tribulation, distress, persecution, famine, nakedness, peril and sword. To be a conqueror, you have to conquer something.

Hebrews 10:9 says, contrasting burnt offerings with submission to God's will, that God "takes away the first that He may establish the second." There are times when God Himself comes into our lives and takes away what we have in order to position us to believe Him for something more. When adversity looms large in our faces, the natural response is to turn inward, to circle the wagons. But David exclaimed to God in Psalm 4:1, "You have relieved me when I was in distress." Even in the hardest of times, even after the greatest of setbacks, God expects us to respond to His call and to continue moving forward.

Can we apply that principle to the cultural captivity of the contemporary Church? It would seem that God wants us to change. Do we agree that we do not need to recover the good old days? If they were as good as we like to remember, our society would probably not be in the decline it is currently. Some Christians engage in revisionist history-making. In the 1940s and 1950s, for example, although the Church had a tremendous influence on every aspect of society, it was not as perfect as some remember it. They forget the racism, the apathy for the poor, the religious formalism that masked the absence of true spirituality.

"Mission is the mother of theology," wrote Martin Kahler in 1909. "In exile, the Jews were forced to be bilingual; they developed the synagogue; they recovered the doctrine of angels as globally significant ministering spirits (see Daniel 9), a doctrine virtually unneeded and unheeded back in Jerusalem."[8]

God's purpose from the beginning was for the Jews to return from captivity to their own land where they could rebuild the Temple and reinstitute Judaism as the focal point of society and culture. The purpose, however, was not just to restore these touchpoints, but to reestablish them with a new and improved attitude. God does not just want to restore the influence of the Church in America; He wants to *change* the Church in America. Listening to the way some Christians talk about restoration is a little scary—scary because it seems we did not learn much about humility in our captivity, or learn the lesson the first time around as we watched our best and brightest being led away in shackles. God just might prefer we stay there a little longer.

*Lesson 4: Captivity Always Produces Equal Measures
of Devastation and Opportunity*

History records that Nebuchadnezzar invaded Judah on three occasions. After the first invasion, Daniel was taken captive to Babylon. After the second, Ezekiel was taken. And after the third, Ezra and Nehemiah were taken.

Captivity always produces equal measures of devastation and opportunity. The word for *crisis* in Chinese is made up of two symbols. The top character represents potential danger; the lower conveys hidden opportunity. Together they convey the idea that every crisis presents the potential for peril and providence. The results of a crisis depend on how we respond to it. Many people are emotionally and spiritually debilitated by personal challenges and never arise to triumph over them. Others who capitalize on what seem to be insignificant opportunities that arise during their captivity qualify themselves for promotion to greatness.

Joseph, who made the journey from the pit to the palace without bitterness of soul and spirit, learned to triumph over adversity. King David went, in a relatively short period of time, from herding his father's flocks to hiding in a cave to sitting on the throne, ruling the tribes of Israel. Esther, who rose from captive to queen, was used by God to save her people from genocide. The apostle Paul wrote many of the New Testament epistles shackled in a filthy dungeon. Jesus laid aside His royalty and took the form of a bondservant. In this lowly state He earned from the Father the privilege to be King of kings and Lord of lords. He, more than all others, capitalized on His captivity.

All these seemed to understand the Hebrew concept of crisis. The Hebrew word for crisis, *mashber,* is also used to describe a birth stool, the seat on which a Jewish woman sat as she gave birth. Your crisis can become the birthing ground for unrealized destiny.

What are you doing with the limitations of life? Do you use them to get better, or are you allowing the devastation of captivity to make you bitter? The opportunities are usually difficult to recognize. Generally the occasions that provide a ticket to freedom and a position of influence over our captors are small ones that seem to carry no promise. That is why God uses captivity as a means of testing. It sorts out the truly faithful from those who just want to be more comfortable. Those who are faithful in the little things, whether or not these appear to be opportunities, have stumbled onto the keys to their freedom.

Are you taking advantage of the doors God opens, or have you settled in, learning to live within the boundaries of your captivity?

The Prospects for a Comeback

When we consider where we are as a culture today, in a state of decline, we might ask the question, How did we get here? Was it simply the judgment of God, or was it the Church's lack of diligence?

The answer is both. God's sovereignty and our own efforts have always been mysteriously intertwined. Consequently our response to cultural captivity is twofold:

- We must humble ourselves, repent and pray as if the restoration were entirely a sovereign act.
- We must rise up in boldness of faith to take advantage of every opportunity and every open door to reestablish the influence of the Kingdom of God in every part of our culture.

Some say we have gone too far down the road of secularism to return, and that, as a consequence, God has given up on Western culture. To prove their point they cite every imaginable statistic revealing the decline of Western civilization. The underlying assumption is that when a certain percentage of people turn away from God, judgment is inevitable.

But these believers fail to understand that God does not count as we do. Abraham, interceding with God for the city of Sodom, persuaded Him to spare the city for the sake of just ten righteous men! I cannot help but wonder how the Lord would have responded if Abraham had continued to press Him for mercy on account of only one or two. The point is, the ratio of righteous to unrighteous did not matter nearly as much as who it was interceding for them.

By God's grace and power, things can happen that are considered impossible. If you were to make a list of the most remarkable and improbable events of all history, one of them would be the exodus from Egypt after four hundred years of slavery. Another would be the restoration of the Jews from Babylonian captivity.

With these events in mind, wouldn't it be a relatively small thing for God to revive and restore Western society, even if such revival might be considered, by human effort alone, a cultural impossibility? Our setback must become the framework for our comeback.

3

THE CULTURE CONNECTION

> To every man there comes in his lifetime that special moment when he is figuratively tapped on the shoulder and offered that chance to do a special thing, unique to him and fitted to his talents.
>
> Winston Churchill

Sitting in a hot, dusty classroom, Daniel swallowed the bitter taste in his mouth. For the first time since being taken captive, he allowed himself to consider the gravity of his situation. As a representative of the cream of Judah's crop, he had been hand-picked, along with Hananiah, Mishael, Azariah and others, to be trained in the school of the Chaldeans. Rather than being forced into common labor or imprisoned like many of the other captives, he was being schooled to serve the Babylonian king. Thus he was required to learn the Babylonian language, embrace Babylonian customs and negotiate with foreign dignitaries on Nebuchadnezzar's behalf. Daniel was forced to serve the barbarians who had murdered his people.

The school of the Chaldeans was one of the most influential of the ancient world. The most learned instructors of the world staffed this "University of Babylon." In that place were discovered many of the principles of mathematics and astronomy that have become the foundation for modern science. To the Babylonians we owe the exact measurements of the lunar and solar cycles, the tracing of the planets and the designation of the constellations. The science department first interpreted the division of the circle into 360 degrees.

This school was influential in training most of the Babylonian priests, who were revered for their expertise in astrology, divination, magic arts and prophetic predictions. The Chaldean language was considered a sacred tongue that required years of training to master and was used primarily by the elite priesthood of the day.

The pressure to be squeezed into the mold designated by the Babylonians must have been intense. But Daniel resolved at the outset not to be defiled by even the same source of physical nourishment as the Babylonians. Rather than eat the king's meat and drink his wine, he and his friends asked to eat only vegetables and water for ten days, as a test. He was a chosen man on a spiritual assignment in an alien culture. As noted author and youth evangelist Winkie Pratney observes:

> What happened to Daniel has happened again in your time. The pressures they faced and the program they put on is here again. Babylon the ancient city is gone. Babylon the spiritual power of the world never left. Young people on the edge of the 21st century have to deal with Babylon today. You have the same choices Daniel and his three friends had to face. Babylon is alive, dangerous and dominant in the ruling civilizations of our century.[1]

As I walked the halls of the high school recently where Terry, my oldest son, had just been enrolled as a freshman, I was confronted with how out of touch I was with the youth culture. All those tattooed teenagers, pierced navels and fluorescent hair colors looked like the nightclub scene in the movie *Star Wars*! My parental instincts were screaming at me to grab Terry by the arm and run for the closest door before either of us was contaminated with some social virus. After several deep breaths and a quiet prayer, however, I continued on my way to the high school cafeteria.

Now, several months later, I have begun the process of identifying the spiritual needs of those teenagers without being overwhelmed by the outlandish dress and peculiar behavior of some of the more flamboyant ones. Through listening and learning, I have come to discover that the young people of this generation are only reflecting what they have learned by the example (or neglect) of their parents. Even though many parents would like to blame them for our social ills, we must face the fact that they have not determined their culture; we have.

We are locked in mortal combat with this abstract, mysterious adversary called "culture." To most people the concept of culture is vague. One person equates culture with the mysterious incantations of the medicine man in a Native American rain dance. To a biologist culture refers to bacteria growing in a petri dish. A corporate executive defines organizational culture as "the way we do things around here." To my wife, culture is expressed through classical music, art and poetry.

"Culture is like the air we breathe," writes distinguished theologian Charles Sherlock. "Unless we are ill or are making a deliberate attempt to concentrate on it, breathing is something we take for granted. So it is with culture; unless we deliberately focus upon it, or move to live in another culture, we are largely unaware that we are 'cultured.'"[2]

For the sake of this book, I have chosen to define *culture* as the prevailing value system of a group of people as expressed through politics, education, economics, art, media, entertainment, athletics and science. Culture is the prevalent expression of human life within the context of a nation, region or particular ethnicity in society.

For human cultures to survive (let alone thrive), they must possess an internal element of cohesiveness. These are the bonding agents that empower individuals to develop a sense of common identity—social elements that cause people to think as "we" rather than "me." Distinctive people groups usually organized themselves around geography and language; eventually they developed into nations.

But if proximity and language are the only common bonds, large people groups quickly disintegrate into little warring factions unless they share a set of core values that evolve from a common belief system. The most powerful and resilient among those are religious values based on devout convictions. Consequently every culture develops from and with an associated religion.

Ray Sutton gives an excellent definition of *culture* in his insightful book *That You May Prosper:*

> There are no sacred/profane categories inherent in creation. The original garden had zones that were nearer to and further away from God, but everything everywhere was sacred. Corporate man, male and female, was to spread culture. What is culture? "Culture" comes from *cultus,* meaning worship. Thus [we are] . . . to transform the world into a place of worship, and thereby create true culture . . . [We are] making society into a proper place to worship God.[3]

Culture is the materialistic way a people express their religion. Professor Allan Bloom writes, "The very idea of culture was a way of preserving something like religion without talking about it. Culture is the synthesis of reason and religion, attempting to hide the sharp distinction."[4]

All cultures are "religious." As you analyze any given society, you realize you are looking at the idolatrous image of what people bow before, even if it is not easy to identify those gods. Even atheistic societies have religious core values, in the sense that they encourage the worship of a philosophy or worldview—a godless religion. The outworking of their value system, whatever it may be, is revealed in all aspects of daily life. We cannot separate culture from religion, because the essence of culture is the expression of the people's religious value system. Having spent a significant portion of my life ministering outside the United States, I have had my eyes opened to see our own national religion—the worship of independence, success and materialism.

Many people miss the religious overtones of their own cultures simply because they have no other frame of reference. Their proximity to the problem impairs their ability to discern the danger. It is always easier to identify spiritual strongholds in foreign nations, especially in countries where no attempt has been made to hide the connection between religion and culture.

Professor Bloom continues, "A shared sense of the sacred is the surest way to recognize a culture, and the key to understanding it and all its facets. . . . What a people bows before tells us what it is."[5] It does not take great discernment to discover that India is what it is largely due to the influence of Hinduism. The same identity connection exists between China and Buddhism, Arabic nations and Islam, the West and Christianity. If you are not convinced that religion is the essence of culture, ask any dictator or senior party official of a totalitarian state. Those who seek to control people groups never leave religion alone. Whatever their brand of tyranny—Communist, Nazi, Babylonian—the essence of control is culture, and the essence of culture is religion.

Since religion lies at the very root of culture, it is the slowest and most difficult aspect of culture to change. Is it hard to see why the political, educational and entertainment powers of the Western world formally disassociated from Christianity several decades ago? It has taken many years, however, for the culture to degenerate at the grassroots level. Judge Robert H. Bork wrote:

> Some few years ago friends whose judgment I greatly respect argued that religion constitutes the only reliable basis for morality and that when religion loses its hold on a society, standards of morality will gradually crumble. I objected that there were many moral people who are not at all religious; my friends replied that such people are living on the moral capital left by generations that believed there is a God and that He makes demands on us. The prospect, they said, was that the remaining moral capital would dwindle and our societies become less moral.[6]

Christ in Culture

Almost fifty years have passed since H. Richard Niebuhr published his classic study on *Christ in Culture*. Niebuhr, a German Reformed theologian, listed five different options Christians have in relating to culture.

- Christ against culture
- Christ of culture
- Christ above culture
- Christ and culture in paradox
- Christ transforming culture[7]

Let me offer a brief synopsis of these five different options.

1. Essential Opposition: Christ Against Culture

Generally speaking, "Christ against culture" has been the view of most evangelicals throughout the past century. Because of the wickedness abounding in the earth, Christ is opposed (in this viewpoint) to all forms of human culture. The Church is a "peculiar people" with zero tolerance for anything that appears worldly. Music, dance, drama and many other artistic expressions must, according to this view, be rejected as detrimental to true holiness. Christians are required to discard anything that finds its root or expression in contemporary culture, and to withdraw from society in order to form their own spiritual enclaves, thereby protecting themselves from spiritual defilement.

2. Fundamental Agreement: Christ of Culture

From this perspective the Church and culture are fully compatible. Christ is identified with and fully expressed through contemporary culture. Christians are to be enculturated to the degree that they are indistinguishable from culture. It is not the world that needs to be changed, according to this position, but rather Christianity itself. The Church must be secularized and become the servants of the world's culture. Do we even want to call this view Christian? Perhaps not.

3. Integration: Christ Above Culture

This position is less static than the preceding two, in that Christ is both contiguous and discontiguous with human culture. This balance between separation and accommodation places Christians in harmony with culture but prepared to withstand culture as the need arises. This view begins with a biblical understanding of the Kingdom of God—that is, Jesus Christ is Lord over all and desires to be personally present, through the agency of the Holy Spirit, and governing the affairs of humanity. The danger to avoid is when men consider the Church coequal with Christ in His sovereignty over the nations. This view set the stage for papal supremacy in the Middle Ages.

4. Tension: Christ and Culture in Paradox

Niebuhr referred to this fourth option as dualism because it affirms the dual citizenship of every Christian, who is at once a member of the city of God and the city of man. Neither city is to take precedence over the other, as each serves a different purpose in the affairs of humanity. In this view culture and religion operate in different spheres of authority without effecting change in one another. This position proved difficult to maintain during the Nazi oppression of World War II. The danger here is that of dividing life into two distinct and separate spheres—the sacred and the secular.

5. Conversion: Christ Transforming Culture

The final option is that of transformation, or social conversion. This is the position Niebuhr seemed to favor. Christ saves and converts people within their own culture, then moves them toward the process of bringing all of culture under the Lordship of Jesus Christ.

This, I believe, is the present prophetic mission of the Church. We are called to penetrate the hardened soil of society with the Gospel of the Kingdom, thereby bringing revival, restoration and reformation. The Church is the leaven that works faithfully, patiently and tirelessly in society to transform it according to the will of God. We must accept the responsibility to make a difference in the realms of politics, family, religion, media, entertainment and economics.

In spite of the contribution of this priceless work, most Christians still need a broader understanding of the role of the Church in relationship to contemporary culture. The primary weakness in

Niebuhr's overview is that it tends toward oversimplification. It forces us to choose one static response, rather than respond dynamically based on the disposition of culture toward Christ. Each of these positions (with the exception of integration) have probably been appropriate at one time or another in history, based on society's attitudes at that time toward Christianity.

In light of postmodernism, which tolerates but does not elevate Christianity, I believe the appropriate position for the twenty-first-century Church is one of *conversion*. Postmodernism is as difficult to define as it is to choose just one flavor at your local Baskin-Robbins. It is the worldview that denies all other worldviews. At the core of postmodernism is the belief that all truth is relative and that absolutes do not exist. To the postmodern mind, Jesus Christ is accepted as one path to eternal life, never the only way. And we have been given the opportunity to affect, reform and even transform this mindset!

Keeping Pace with the Competition

When the computer in my car began talking to me, and the local cable company expanded my service to 83 different channels, I knew there was no turning back. By far the most dominating aspect of the 1990s was the speed of communication and the accessibility of information. We rapidly approached the place of instant access to every other human on the planet, as well as to the entire record of human knowledge.

We live in an era when time and space are being compressed geometrically. Fast, inexpensive transportation, along with satellite telecommunications, means that there are, in effect, no faraway places. If war breaks out in the desert of Saudi Arabia, residents of Iowa can sit in their living rooms with a live, front-line view of the battle. Can you imagine having watched the D-Day invasion of Normandy on *CNN Live,* or having tuned in as T. S. Lawrence led a cavalry charge riding a camel? The world is being electronically compressed into such a small place that we have a real-time visual connection with even obscure events in the most remote places.

We are also seeing all information in exponential development, when the concept of "up-to-date" data is so temporary as to be irrelevant. The same is happening with culture time; we are witnessing the rapid compression of social progression. The speed by which we move from one identifiable generation to the next is proportionate to the increased speed of information and communication in the twenty-first century. The half-life of cultural language and trends is getting so short that if a youth worker takes a yearlong sabbatical, he struggles on his return to relate culturally to what kids are talking about.

Consider this example. The Middle Ages are generally considered to span five hundred years. The Victorian Era lasted from 1837 to 1908. The so-called "matures," born between 1909 and 1945, came of age under the shadows of the Great Depression, World War II, Korea and the Cold War. Baby boomers were born between 1946 and 1964. And in less than forty years since then, we have identified not one but two succeeding generations, Generation X and Generation Y. Time is being crunched.

Whenever there is rapid social and cultural change, there are groups and individuals who simply drop out, either because they are unable to keep up or because they do not like the changes and have given up fighting them. They usually retreat into a counter-cultural group or lifestyle to proclaim the virtues of old-fashioned, simple living. For religious people this has taken the form of various kinds of monastic movements.

A lot of good can be said about retreating from the rat race. One of the great dangers of the twenty-first century, however, is that the Church may continue to retreat to the cultural sidelines and revert to an expression of Christianity that prides itself in irrelevance. Many churches have already dropped out of the culture war because of sheer exhaustion!

Another challenge for the Church is the battle for truth, in which the rules of evidence are changing. The raging flood of information has not necessarily made people smarter. As newspaper columnist Charlie Reese once wrote in *The Orlando Sentinel,* "The irony is that just as the technology of communications has reached its superb height, the task of sorting fact from fiction has gotten more difficult instead of easier." More words, more entertainment, more commercial propaganda—but less real truth.

Even historical truth is not what it used to be. Revisionists are rewriting history in order to advance their own social and political causes. To compound the problem, we have also experienced the trend toward the disconnection of history from truth altogether by teaching *what if* historical scenarios. The objective is not so much to discover what actually happened, but to discuss questions such as, *What if* Washington had surrendered at Valley Forge? *What if* the American aircraft carriers had been anchored at Pearl Harbor on December 7, 1941? *What if* Christ had not been born?

If you think there is an obvious good or evil in the answers to these questions, you are way out of touch with how kids are being taught to think today. But it is in this cultural and intellectual environment that the Church must train people to think in terms of timeless, absolute truth based on historical evidence.

It is difficult for most matures to relate to teenagers today. The youth culture seems too bizarre for them to comprehend. Their generation carried the country on their backs through a lot of hard times and saved the world from Hitler. They feel they deserve some respect, and resent the fact that they do not get much from the younger generation.

It is true that they deserve respect. But let's face it, many "generational newcomers" are not really into respect. So if this generation is to find a connection with the previous generation that evokes a righteous mentoring, then older folks had better swallow their pride and make the first move to create an environment of restoration and healing. That is what it will take to connect with today's offspring in order to see generational transformation.

Engaging the Culture

When asked to identify the number-one problem in the Church, Dr. E. Stanley Jones, the esteemed Methodist missionary and critical thinker, confidently replied, "Irrelevance!" Although he did not consider the Gospel to be inherently irrelevant, Dr. Jones did believe that Christians were failing to show in practical ways how Jesus Christ is relevant to life at the end of the twentieth century.

We must face the fact that in the battle for the hearts, souls and minds of Generations X and Y, the competition is getting tougher. Consider this: If the Church was struggling with irrelevance thirty years ago, what is our condition today and what will our position be twenty years from now? The time to engage the culture for the sake of spiritual and social transformation is *now.* Tomorrow may be too late.

But how do we do it? And what does it even mean to be a relevant Christian in the midst of cultural quicksand?

Let's begin with the word itself. The Latin root *relevare* simply means "to bear upon." Based on that definition, I believe that relevant Christians are those who influence the lives of men and women and the structures of nations. Spiritual relevance is the act of communicating truth in such a way that it has personal and practical bearing on its recipients. This challenge, as you can see, is greater than any responsibility to communicate with the foreign nations that live in our very own backyard. We now have to face up to subtle nuances that define cross-cultural missions in the twenty-first century.

Several years ago I was invited to minister in a denominational pastors conference deep in the jungle of South America. Unable to accept the invitation due to a scheduling conflict, I sent one of my associate pastors as a replacement. He returned several weeks later describing a ludicrous instance of cross-cultural noncommunication.

The conference was held in a remote location on the Amazon River. In addition to the ministers attending from the closest city— Lima, Peru—most of the village pastors traveled by dugout canoe for as much as three days to reach the meeting. Many of these leaders had few possessions apart from their battered old Bibles. Some did not even own a pair of shoes.

The other conference speaker was a local Peruvian who had attended Bible college in the United States and had returned recently to minister to his people. His message to those village pastors was on the subject of time management.

"You must buy a pocket organizer," he advised, "and consult it carefully every morning before going to your office."

Most of these village pastors had never stepped foot in an office! Some of their villages only had a handful of people living in primitive conditions.

I still have a difficult time believing how out of touch he had become with his own culture. But perhaps the greater tragedy is that many of us have allowed ourselves to become equally out of touch with our postmodern culture. For a message to be relevant to the postmodern mind, two vital factors must be present. First, *the issue being discussed must have bearing on our lives.* It has to address the challenges we face at this moment in history. It must expose the truth that lies deep beneath our carefully constructed masks of pride and arrogance. But that is not enough. *A message is not relevant to our postmodern culture unless it provides a practical solution to our present dilemma: having gone adrift with no moral compass.*

If we are to survive and even thrive in the twenty-first century, then cultural relevance must become the mission of the Church. Keep in mind that her mandate at every point in history has been to enable those in a particular generation and culture to connect personally with the Gospel message. If they do not, the Church will cease to exist in the next generation. So the mission of the Church is reliant upon how well Christians transmit the Good News across generational and cultural barriers.

This sobering task becomes even greater when you consider that culture and communications are currently changing faster than articles can be written about them. We are on pace to experience a cultural paradigm shift every single decade. That is why I believe this issue alone—effectively communicating in the language of contemporary culture—will be the greatest of all challenges for the Church in this new millennium.

Prospects for Victory

Now for the good news. While many Christians are pessimistic about their ability to influence the direction of American culture, those who vehemently oppose Christianity see things differently. They take into account the number of churches, Christian schools and universities, Christian radio and TV stations; the billions of dollars in contributions to thousands of Christian nonprofit organizations; and the individual Christians infiltrating every aspect of society. And they are horrified at the thought! I wish Christians would be so optimistic about their own potential.

Amid a lot of good news to focus on, let me briefly define four of the basic principles about which the Church can be encouraged. Let's call these principles "Kingdom Power Points."

Power Point 1: The Power of God Is Contained within the Gospel

Whenever the Gospel is communicated in the language of the common person, the power of the Holy Spirit is present to transform people's lives.

The apostle Paul had his own cultural hurdles to leap over. He labored in a cultural environment that was a long way from Jerusalem. As a Pharisee, philosopher and religious intellectual, he was challenged with planting the Gospel in a Gentile culture filled with all kinds of pagan assumptions. How did he succeed? Because Christ sent him "to preach the gospel, not with wisdom of words, lest the cross of Christ should be made of no effect. For the message of the cross is foolishness to those who are perishing, but to us who are being saved it is the power of God" (1 Corinthians 1:17–18).

Whether bringing about physical miracles, the testimony of a transformed life or the work of the Holy Spirit in a person's heart, the power of God drives the spreading of the Gospel. We can eliminate entire portions of the Good News in order to make the message more "palatable" to postmodern seekers, but to do so is to remove the transforming power of the message. When you tell someone about Jesus Christ, it is not just the power of your argument, but the influence of the Holy Spirit working in and through the message, that can change that person's life.

I am sure you have heard testimonies of how the simplest comment brought someone to Christ through the Holy Spirit's conviction. Becoming a Christian is more than changing one's belief system. It is experiencing a transformation of the inner person by the active presence of God's Spirit.

Power Point 2: We Do Not Need to Reinvent the Message of the Gospel

In fact, that is the worst thing the Church can do! Every church or ministry that tries to relate to a particular culture, whether inner-city youth or sophisticated suburbanites, must ask itself this question: Is the purpose of God the force behind the endeavor, or is the pressure of postmodern culture diluting the message? We are in danger of obscuring the Gospel for the sake of being culturally inoffensive. If our primary goal is to make it painless for a post-modern audience to come to Christ, just where do we draw the line between the negotiables and the nonnegotiables? Do we eliminate the biblical values of repentance, submission, obedience, morality, serving and giving?

It still costs to carry the cross. When the radical nature of New Testament Christianity is diluted in an attempt at cultural relevance, the power of spiritual transformation is lost.

I believe our definition of relevance is in desperate need of reworking. In his masterful work *The Unshakable Kingdom and the Unchanging Person,* Dr. E. Stanley Jones wrote, "If the Kingdom of God is missing in the magnificent and in the minute, then the key to meaning, goal, life-redemption and life-fulfillment is missing. But if you have the key of the Kingdom, you find it a master key, the key to life now and hereafter, life individual and collective. And that is important to the modern man: You have the key to relevancy in every situation."[8]

Without an understanding of the rule and reign of Jesus Christ, we are doomed to irrelevance in spite of our greatest intention and most noble effort. It is impossible to connect with and transform a generation apart from teaching the Lordship of Jesus Christ. The Kingdom of God is the moral compass giving us a directional reading on where we presently are in light of where we should be.

We do not have to make the Kingdom of God "relevant" to fallen man at all. The rule and reign of Jesus is the only reality that can ever answer the heart cry of man to be loved, valued and nurtured.

God's Kingdom is the only truth that gives purpose and meaning to life. God's Kingdom is the only sure foundation in the midst of cultural quicksand.

Nor do we have to make the Bible relevant. It has always been and will always be. As Carl F. H. Henry once stated, "The Christian belief system, which the Christian knows to be grounded in Divine revelation, is relevant to all of life."[9] The Word of God contains the key to life in every generation, among every socioeconomic class and in every tongue, tribe and nation. It is our religious opinions, personal convictions and spiritual preferences that often obscure the truth, making it appear irrelevant to the very ones we are trying to reach.

We must labor to make the Church relevant. History has proven that only without the progressive outworking of the rule and reign of Christ is the Church irrelevant. The Kingdom of God, not the Church, is the leaven that leavens the whole lump. And when the Church refuses to embrace the principles of Kingdom living, she becomes stagnant, introverted, encumbered and institutional. Conversely, when she embraces the principles of the Kingdom, she is driven by her very outworking into society. Theology always precedes methodology.

Effective cross-cultural communication of the Gospel is accomplished, first, by scraping away the barnacles of nonessential religious tradition that have attached themselves to us over time. In other words, eliminate the stuff that obscures the fundamental essence of Christianity in the minds of nonreligious people. This can mean, among other things, practices carried on out of habit. Secondary theological issues. Religious jargon that makes no sense outside the walls of your church.

For most young ministers in my denomination, the word *God* became a Southern-twanged two-syllable word. It may have worked in the pulpit but it sounded ridiculous anywhere else. A few years ago I had little cultural empathy, like many of the people to whom I was preaching. I did not realize how my words sounded in the ears of nonbelievers.

We need to be careful not to let our cultural captivity reshape the identity of the Church and the character of worship. The religion of the Pharisees is a good example.

The form of Judaism into which Jesus was born emerged first in Babylon. Among the captives in that foreign land, the question arose, "Since we can't go to the Temple in Jerusalem, how do we worship?" So it was that during Judah's captivity, the concept of the local synagogue developed. Before Babylon the Jews focused on the Temple, the sacrifices and the priests. After Babylon their attention shifted to the synagogue, the Law and the lawyers (the scribes and Pharisees). What developed as a result: a brand of Judaism that was highly legalistic. The lawyers who ran it added countless rules and regulations that defined righteousness in almost completely external terms. How the Jews allowed their captivity to shape their worship was what provoked Jesus to pronounce judgment on them.

The challenge for the Church in cultural captivity is to make the Gospel relevant to the Babylonians without allowing her captivity to change the essence of true faith and worship.

Power Point 3: The Light of the Gospel Is Magnified in the Darkest Place

Every generation since the birth of the Church has harbored those who have tried to extinguish Christianity by brute force. It has just never succeeded. Making circumstances as difficult as possible for believers has only provided a stage on which the Holy Spirit displayed the power of the Gospel in a more dramatic manner.

Don't misunderstand me; no one should desire persecution. But there is a purpose for every challenge we encounter in life. At this point in history the Church must quickly take advantage of the opportunities before they disappear.

Jesus compared our influence on the world to a lit lamp. "Don't put it under a bushel basket," He warned (to paraphrase Matthew 5:15). People who have been isolated in a dark room for a long time squint and shade their eyes at the brightness of even a very small light. As the world we live in becomes darker, more chaotic and more devoid of character and values, it becomes easier for us to be a dynamic light and witness for Christ. You don't have to perform extraordinary spiritual feats. Just being a normal Christian is radical in the eyes of those around you.

Power Point 4: When You Open the Gates to the Kingdoms of This World, the King of Glory Will Come In!

A redeemed people empowered with the Holy Spirit and in possession of the Word of God are the most significant of all cultural influences. This is true in every generation. A little bit leavens the whole lump. The Gospel and the Kingdom of God are the immovable rock that remains solid through every cultural change; through unprecedented prosperity and freedom as well as through captivity. There are great opportunities for the Church issuing directly from the unique culture in which we live. The speed of change and the growth of technology create a whole new service industry— that of answering questions about meaning, purpose, truth and eternity. For the Church it is the perfect situation.

Jesus, Lord of Culture

Our mission as sons and daughters of the Kingdom is to demonstrate the Lordship of Jesus Christ, thereby influencing culture for the sake of righteousness. In Psalm 2:8 the Father invites the Son to "ask of Me, and I will give You the nations for Your inheritance, and the ends of the earth for Your possession." The Lordship of Jesus Christ has had a transforming effect on society wherever and whenever it has been demonstrated.

Human culture was originally designed to express the reality of God in all His sovereignty and glory. When man fell into sin, the power to fulfill this mandate was lost. But in Jesus Christ it has been restored, *and the submission of nations to the Lordship of Jesus Christ in every sphere of life will lead to the transformation of human culture.*

Jesus Christ did not enter humanity, robed in the limitation of sinful flesh, just to join in with our way of living. He came to take over, transform and redirect the affairs of humanity. The Father gave Him the nations of the earth (in their present cultural condition), knowing that under Christ's government and rule, divine order will be established. This is not the commission to simply throw out the lifeline and rescue the perishing. It is the mandate to transform the nations with the Word of God.

Isaiah saw this day through the light of prophetic vision:

> Arise, shine; for thy light is come, and the glory of the LORD is risen upon thee. For, behold, the darkness shall cover the earth, and gross darkness the people: but the LORD shall arise upon thee, and his glory shall be seen upon thee. And the Gentiles [or nations] shall come to thy light, and kings to the brightness of thy rising.
>
> Isaiah 60:1–3, KJV

The more you consider this principle, the clearer Matthew 28:19 becomes: "Make disciples of the nations." It is inadequate to tell men simply to believe in Christ; we must tell them to believe Christ *and* obey Him in all areas of life. As with Daniel, I believe that God is positioning individual Christians, and the Church as a whole, to get engaged in the battle for cultural influence. As the earthly representatives of the Kingdom of God, we are responsible to implement and administer the dictates of King Jesus.

Listen to what Matthew Henry, the great theologian and Bible commentator, once said regarding Matthew 28:

> What is the principal intention of this commission; to *disciple* all nations. *Matheteusate*—*"Admit them disciples;* do your utmost to make the nations Christian nations."* . . . Christ the Mediator is setting up a Kingdom in the world, bring up the nations to be His subjects; setting up a school, bring the nations to be His scholars; raising an army for carrying on the war against the powers of darkness; enlisting the nations of the earth under His banner.[10]

The missiological responsibility of Matthew 28:19 requires that we communicate the message of salvation as well as social justice. God wants to build an altar in every aspect of society, a spiritual dwelling place, a site of worship where His glory can be revealed, where men will acknowledge Him as the Source of everything good and perfect. This is the key to the spiritual and social reclamation of the earth.

No, every individual will not be saved, because men and women possess the power of choice, and many will choose to walk the broad path of destruction. But whole tribes and countries will experience the leavening effect of the Church in her mission to reach the lost and transform the culture. This is the reformation of the nations as we see them delivered from the disorder of tyranny, injustice and oppression in order to be brought into the order of life, liberty and justice.

Challenging This Generation

Now that the Church finds herself in a post-Christian society, what are we to do with the captivity in which we find ourselves? Will we whine away our days in frustration, or open our eyes to the opportunities God is offering us?

We are living in a day of the restructuring of nations, of the transformation of cultures. As I travel throughout the nations, I am constantly reminded that this is the greatest time of opportunity and advancement in the history of man. But many of us believers seem to be waiting around for the enemy to retreat before we begin laying hands on the sick, casting out demons, clothing the poor and doing the works of Jesus. We seem to be waiting for a safe and secure environment, without real threat of retaliation, before taking on the social challenges of the day. We will never change a generation, however, until we are willing to risk it all.

God is issuing a mandate for His people to disciple the nations with the Word of God. He is looking for radical followers who will arise and step beyond the limitations of previous, powerless generations. He is looking for Daniels who will get involved and make a difference, who will take back everything stolen by the work of the enemy. The time has come to reclaim the arts and sciences, politics and economics, education and athletics, industry and commerce. As long as we are comfortable in our current cultural captivity, we will never change a generation or touch the world for Christ.

Little happens without real leadership. The Church needs pioneers who are not just telling others what they ought to do, but are stepping out in front to cut a path through rugged terrain. This means pastors, but it also means elders, deacons, Sunday school teachers and people who work in the private sector.

I cannot help noting that the real leadership in Babylon came from those serving in secular areas. Had it not been for a few young Jews in Babylon determined to seize the opportunity of their captivity, Judah would have faded into oblivion, just as Israel had three hundred years earlier. That was not the plan of God the Father. He uses people of character willing to be His instruments. Daniel and his friends realized that in order to honor God in a pagan culture, they had to position themselves for dominion.

On the heels of a dark period in the history of the Church, the great revivalist Charles Finney penned these challenging words:

> The Christian Church was designed to make aggressive movements in every direction—to lift up her voice and put forth her energies against iniquity in high and low places—to reform individuals, communities, and governments, and never rest until the Kingdom, and the greatness of the Kingdom under the whole heaven, shall be given to the saints of the most high God, till every form of iniquity is driven from the earth.[11]

Captivity is often the catalyst for change. It offers us the opportunity to awaken, replenish our strength and arise with renewed purpose. When we begin to see the potential for revival, restoration and reformation; the opportunity to reach the lost, plant churches and reach university campuses; and the prospect of taking back the wealth of the nations; we will be dissatisfied with sitting complacent in our captivity. And we will not miss the opportunity God is issuing to an entire generation—the possibility for a culture connection.

4

THIS IS NOT YOUR FATHER'S WORLDVIEW

The task of Christian leadership is to confront
modern man with the Christian world life view. . . .
Carl F. H. Henry

An excited buzz swept throughout the halls of the University of Babylon. After ten days of intense scrutiny, the test reports had just been posted. Shocked by the results, the prestigious panel of scholars, magicians, astrologers and eunuchs that had been assembled for the testing seemed bewildered. How was it possible that the four princes of Judah, who had been consuming vegetables and water rather than the king's choice meat and wine, looked healthier and more robust than those who feasted at the king's table? To make matters worse, Nebuchadnezzar determined the young Jewish men to be ten times wiser than the magicians and astrologers of his kingdom. What was the secret to their wisdom and understanding?

Daniel watched their heated discussion with amusement. He was proud of his friends. The pressure had been intense. At one point in the examination process, the questions had been directed with such rapid fire that the force of the examination stunned him. The Babylonian scholars would have been shocked to know that he, Daniel, had been trained for this moment from the time he was a child, soaking in the ways of God in the Temple in Jerusalem. There the scribes and elders had taught him the Law, and the prophets had stretched his mind to new levels of understanding, forming his Hebraic worldview.

Daniel's wisdom was not his own. It was the wisdom of another world. It was the perspective of heaven.

Seeing Beyond the Obvious

In order to understand the culture of Babylon, we must understand the spiritual, moral and philosophical values exhibited by modern Babylonians. Contrary to what some moral relativists believe, we cannot divorce our value system from our actions and lifestyle. What we believe determines what we do and how we respond to the challenges and opportunities we face each day. Ideas have consequences, which means that your personal worldview predisposes you toward certain behaviors.

Every individual has a worldview. It may have been constructed consciously or it may simply be the product of our environment, but it governs our behavior. Proverbs 23:7 declares, "[As a man] thinks in his heart, so is he." Your worldview creates certain presuppositions that either motivate or restrict your personal behavior.

Thus is your behavior rooted in your sense of identity. Even though humanism seeks to deconstruct life on every level, spiritual disconnection is nothing more than a figment of our darkened imaginations. Your past cannot be disconnected from your future. Your history cannot be disconnected from your destiny. Your attitudes cannot be disconnected from your personal outcome. And your worldview invariably creates certain presuppositions.

Simply put, a worldview is *the interpretive lens through which you perceive the whole of life.* It is like a pair of eyeglasses through which you view the world, in both seen and unseen dimensions. These lenses give definition and meaning to all you look at—shaping, coloring and interpreting the world around you. You process everything, whether you are conscious of it or not, through these philosophical eyeglasses that represent your value system. Your worldview functions as a filter, an interpretive grid that networks your various and assorted views about how life is to be lived.

Distinguished Harvard scholar Samuel Huntington purports that the world is divided not by geographic boundaries as much as by our religious and cultural traditions—our worldview.[1] A worldview, according to Dr. David Noebel, is "any ideology, philosophy, theology, movement, or religion that provides an overarching approach to understanding God, the world, and man's relations to God and the world."[2]

Although every religion has a particular perspective on the world, few people are consistent in the way they view all the matters of life. Most people fall into the trap of spiritual syncretism, blending multiple worldviews with just enough spirituality thrown in for good measure.

Modernism, which began roughly in the 1700s and ended in the 1950s, was the interpretive lens that magnified science, reason and objective knowledge. The modernist perceives humans as nothing more than physical creatures without spiritual, moral or eternal dimensions. His is a naturalistic approach to life. Blinded to the spiritual domain, he sees nothing beyond the realm of his five senses. Because the physical world is the sum total of reality, he has eliminated the possibility of eternity. Eating, drinking and making merry are the central purpose of life. If one cannot interact with something through the five senses, it has no bearing on his or her existence. The modernist's ability to reason has become his god.

Over the past fifty years, however, postmodernism has become the dominant cultural perspective in the Western world. "*Postmodernism* is a word that has never secured a dictionary definition," says J. I. Packer. "Different people use it in different ways."[3] He goes on to describe a spiritual and intellectual vacuum. "The only agreed-upon element is that postmodernism is a negation of modernism." Perhaps that is why the definitive word in the post-modern vernacular is *whatever.*

Nor is the concept of postmodernism restricted to the philosophical debate. It has infiltrated every aspect of life. As David Wells observes, "Under the post-modern onslaught, all boundaries and distinctions rapidly fall. Some of the losses associated with the collapse of traditional distinctions have been trivial, but others have been earthshaking, and there seems to be no way to distinguish between the two in the post-modern context. People no longer know where the lines fall."[4]

The postmodernist views life through the lens of moral, spiritual and eternal laxity. Nothing is static. Truth is abstract, relative to your situation and subject to whatever feels good for the moment. What you believe to be truth today may not be truth tomorrow. In this philosophical quicksand it is possible to hold opposing views on the very same issue, providing the basis for one to be a Christian Buddhist or a moral stripper. Because the postmodernist believes that all truth is relative and that there are many equal paths leading to eternal life, he behaves in a manner consistent with his worldview. Anything goes.

A biblical worldview, by contrast, is based not on changing times and current cultural indicators but on the eternal Word of God, "a lamp to my feet and a light to my path" (Psalm 119:105). As Edward H. Rain once observed, "Christianity is a world and life view and not simply a series of unrelated doctrines. Christianity includes all of life. Every realm of knowledge, every aspect of life and every facet of the universe find their place and answer within Christianity. It is a system of truth enveloping the entire world in its grasp."[5]

Looking for Truth in All the Wrong Places

Amos 8:11 declares that the days will come when God "will send a famine on the land, not a famine of bread, nor a thirst for water, but of hearing the words of the LORD." Interesting mixed metaphor!—*a famine of hearing.* Knowing the basic drive of human nature to self-preserve, to eat to sustain life, God is essentially saying, "I am going to leave you to your own devices until you feel as though you are starving to hear a word from heaven. Only when you are willing to hear and obey will I open your ears to truth and righteousness."

The culture in which we live fits perfectly into this description. Our generation has rejected truth for so long that many do not even believe in the existence of absolute truth anymore. But that is like denying the existence of dinosaurs simply because we have never seen one, or historical figures because we did not know them personally!

Indeed, there is a famine of hearing the word of the Lord.

Where does truth come from? From one source alone. As the Reformers were accustomed to saying, "All truth is God's truth." When the existence of God is denied, we leave no room for the existence of absolute truth. You cannot believe in God and deny the existence of absolute truth. Conversely you cannot believe in absolute truth and deny the existence of God. The evidence of the moral law—"I helped you, so you have to help me" or "You can't do that to me, it's not fair"—testifies of a Lawgiver. The evidence of judgment suggests the existence of a supreme Judge. The evidence of absolute truth points to One who is true. Truth is not just correct factual information; it is a Person. And truth and God are a package deal. As Francis Schaeffer once stated, "If there are no absolutes beyond man's ideas, then there is no final appeal to judge between individuals and groups whose moral judgments conflict. We are merely left with conflicting opinions."

Unfortunately, many Christians who profess to build their lives on absolute truth have allowed themselves to be influenced by our postmodern culture. As one writer puts it, "We now have our feet firmly planted in mid-air." This spiritual transition is subtle and progressive. As Christians most of us know better than to question whether or not the Bible is the Word of God, because to do so would invalidate the heart of our belief system. But we have fewer reservations about questioning certain tenets within the Bible. We question the doctrines of healing, miracles, judgment, spiritual authority, tithing and many others, which ultimately causes us to develop a "situational theology."

Our generation has fallen into the trap described by one television commercial that encourages the consumer to "question everything." In following that trend, many Christians do not realize there is a difference between searching for truth and cynically demanding that God reveal Himself simply to satisfy our intellectual curiosity.

Searching for truth is the positive, proactive experience of seeking to know the heart and mind of God, using the Bible as guidebook. *Questioning everything* is the critical attitude of demanding that God produce the evidence we want in order to satisfy our cynicism. Searching for truth is an act of faith. Questioning everything is an act of unbelief. Searching for truth is the act of a sensitive heart that wants to please God. Questioning everything is the act of a hardened heart that wants God to please us. When we search for truth, we meet God on His terms. When we question everything, we demand that God meet us on our terms.

After preaching a series of messages recently at an Austrian pastors conference on reclaiming the culture, I had dinner with a group of European leaders. One asked the question, "Based on what you're teaching, where do we begin? The task seems almost overwhelming."

I thought about it for a moment. "In order to recover apostolic Christianity," I ventured, "we need to return to the basics, the foundations of our first-century faith."

They had probably not seen the American television commercial depicting an egg sizzling in a frying pan, which represented "your brain on drugs." But this is where we start with the culture, too: "This is a Bible. This is your brain, on the Bible. Any questions?" Communicating the basics.

Many Christians are being defeated in the arena of ideas because they do not have the basics worked into their lives. They somehow skipped the simple in search of the sensational. Some claim to be authorities on the dynamics of spiritual renewal—the fire of God, the joy of the Lord, signs, wonders and miracles—but they have missed the foundations of basic Christian living. The strength of the groundwork determines the longevity of the structure. If you want to build a life, a marriage or even a ministry, then build a lasting foundation. No structure can exceed the strength of its grounding.

Discovering Spiritual Coherence

More than a hundred years ago, James Orr presented the Kerr Lectures in Edinburgh, Scotland. He entitled his series "The Christian View of God and the World," and argued passionately that Christianity possesses a "view of the world." Even though most Christians consider Christianity relevant only to matters of the heart, Orr believed in God's relevance for the whole of man. "If there is one religion in the world which exalts the office of teaching," he declared, "it is safe to say that it is the religion of Jesus Christ."[6]

In other words, one who says he believes with his whole heart that Jesus Christ is the Son of God "is thereby committed to much else besides." Orr went on to define the scope of that commitment: "He is committed to a view of God, to a view of man, to a view of sin, to a view of redemption, to a view of the purpose of God in creation and history, to a view of human destiny, found only in Christianity."

Perhaps you are wondering, *Isn't this discussion better left to the classrooms of our universities? What does this have to do with my life?* The answer is simple. Again, your actions in life are the product of your worldview. Your choices in life are based on your level of awareness—awareness of truth, of personal identity, even of personal destiny. This is why the enemy blinds us to an understanding of the divine design for our lives. To leave us ignorant is to leave us captive.

Forming the Matrix

One of the blockbuster motion pictures of 1999 was a science fiction movie about the despair of mankind in the late twentieth century. Though somewhat complex at times, the basic plot of *The Matrix* is this: A race of machines, spawned by artificial intelligence, overtakes the planet and begins the process of systematically eliminating those opposed to its diabolical agenda. In an effort to halt the wholesale slaughter of man, the remaining survivors destroy the atmosphere and darken the sky, believing that these solar-powered machines will be rendered useless. Instead the machines find a new source of energy in human body heat, which they begin to harvest in massive power plants. To keep the crop of captive humans from revolting, they are mentally networked into a virtual world called "the matrix," which simulates earth as we currently know it. Eventually someone discovers the truth and manages to free himself before leading a revolt against the status quo. When this revolutionary dies, it is prophesied that he will return, and that his coming will bring an end to the conflict, thereby freeing humanity.

In its opening weekend *The Matrix,* which is based on the search for and discovery of this reincarnated "messiah," earned over fifty million dollars, and it has gone on to sell more copies on DVD than any other movie in the history of the United States and Great Britain. The apparent reason for the popular reception of *The Matrix* among younger audiences: It advocates the removal of all limitations on life, both legislated and self-imposed.

Yet beneath the obvious message of "free your mind"—a double entendre used throughout the film—is a theme that runs much deeper. Did the plot ring a bell? It is impossible to avoid the glaring similarities between the mystical overtones laced throughout the entire movie of a reincarnated "messiah" and the biblical record of redemption.

Arthur Koestler, in his fascinating book *The Act of Creation,* uses the term *matrix* to define the mental filters that enable us to form manageable patterns out of the sensory input we receive in life. He explains that *matrix* "is derived from the Latin word for womb and is figuratively used for any pattern or mold in which things are shaped and developed, or type is cast. Thus, the exercise of a habit or skill is 'molded' by its matrix."[7]

A biblical worldview is also a matrix—a womb that has been carefully constructed out of the principles, patterns and paradigms that are contained within the Scriptures. Without an understanding of these moral absolutes, our lives are rooted in spiritual myth and theological fantasy. The Scriptures are the touchstone of the only valid worldview. I regret having lost the source of the following helpful observation:

> At the center of every worldview is what might be called the "touchstone proposition" of that worldview, a proposition that is held to be the fundamental truth about reality and serves as a criterion to determine which other propositions may or may not count as candidates for belief.

Throughout recent history a touchstone has been used as the standard by which the authenticity of a metal is judged. When old-fashioned gold miners wanted to test the purity of gold or silver, they would scratch the metal in question across the hard surface of the black "touchstone," leaving a scar behind. The purity of the metal was then determined by the color of the scratch left on the stone. Likewise, in the battle for world leadership, every touchstone claims to be the only valid one.

In the final analysis, however, only one worldview will produce the true colors of "righteousness and peace and joy in the Holy Spirit" (Romans 14:17).

The Christian Worldview

There are seven components essential to recognize if we are to develop a biblical worldview.

1. There Is But One True and Sovereign God

The belief that God exists is not unique to the Christian faith. Man has sought to discover and define a Supreme Being throughout the history of religion. Aristotle identified Him as the Prime Mover of the universe. Plato described Him as *It*. Cosmic humanism teaches that God is not a personal Being, but that we are all individual gods and will ascend to rulership to the degree that we have allowed the "Christ consciousness" to rid us of our old, restrictive beliefs. So, which is it?

"What we believe about God," said A. W. Tozer, "is the most important thing about us." Our understanding of God, no matter how limited, inevitably translates itself into our action, attitudes and even worldview. Our awareness of God, therefore, must go beyond the warm, fuzzy idea that He exists in an abstract, impersonal manner. Without an awareness of, and interaction with, the triune God, man is destined to live a diminished, subnormal life.

Rather, the existence of God as a personal Being is what frames the purpose of man. When you reject God as a personal Being, you have eliminated the personal purpose of man as well. Our existence is eternally linked to His.

One of the most challenging aspects of the Christian worldview is the belief that God can and does reveal Himself, so that mankind can really know Him. He revealed Himself first through *general revelation* (in creation), then through *special revelation* (the Scriptures), and ultimately in *the Person of Jesus Christ*. The Word of God contains the self-disclosure of this personal Being who authoritatively reveals His nature and His ways.

2. Evil Is Present and Unavoidable in the World

The greatest enemy of the human race is Satan and the forces of darkness. But many moral relativists consider belief in the existence of a personal devil as naïve, unsophisticated, even primitive. This view has resulted partly as a reaction to unbiblical and unhealthy poetic expressions about Satan during the Middle Ages. In any case, many today have swung to the opposite extreme, denying the personal existence of Satan altogether.

But in spite of our blindness to the work of evil in the world, Satan lives with the agenda of destroying everything God intended for His pleasure. Although he does not possess the same qualities as God (omniscience, omnipotence and omnipresence), he has progressively filled the earth with spiritual darkness.

The romantic notion of living in relationship with Jesus Christ as a way of avoiding the challenges of life is dangerous. The Scriptures teach the opposite. To live righteously is to invite the wrath of the kingdom of darkness. The quality of our lives can be measured by the degree of resistance we muster to the kingdom of darkness.

We have been given the power we need to overcome Satan and his minions. The only way out of temptations, testings and trials is to plow through them, knowing we can be of good cheer because Jesus Christ has "overcome the world" (John 16:33). Therefore, "whatever is born of God overcomes the world" (1 John 5:4).

3. The Mercy of God Is Freely Offered to Man

Many people picture God through the lens of deism—distant, aloof, indifferent to the needs of mortals until we can somehow move Him to action through our desperate cries of pain.

The Bible, by contrast, reveals a sovereign God who, long before we ever sinned in the Garden of Eden, had already taken the initiative to map out the redemption of man. It was man, not God, who initiated separation in the Garden of Eden. But it was God, not man, who initiated mercy following that separation. Although fallen man is undeserving, the mercy of God is offered freely to him through the life of Jesus Christ, thereby reinstituting fellowship with God.

The mercy of God also serves as a pattern of the way we are to interact with one another, and with the unregenerate, as sons and daughters of the Kingdom.

4. Man Is Chosen, Fallen and Redeemed

"What is man?" asked the psalmist David three thousand years ago (Psalm 8:4). This question has never been fully satisfied for the postmodern seeker. Are we nothing more than the product of colliding dust particles? Are we the final result of ascending apes? Are we anything more than what we see in the physical dimension?

God designed you and me to live in righteousness, but we were shaped in iniquity and conceived in sin (see Psalm 51:5). Although we were created to rule and reign, we entered life as slaves to unrighteousness.

All men, saved and unsaved, hold a place of extreme worth in the heart of God. But we must accept the fact that there is a fundamental difference between fallen man and redeemed man. It is one thing to be created by God, and quite another to live in relationship with Him and allow Him to father us. Man is chosen, fallen and redeemed. Where we choose to live in regard to those three options is up to you and me.

5. Jesus Christ Is the Only Path to Eternal Life

Two thousand years ago the birth of Jesus Christ divided time and opened the door to eternity. His birth changed the world forever. It does not matter what you think about René Descartes or Friedrich Nietzsche; it does matter what you believe about Jesus Christ.

In recent years magazines, newspapers and television programs have documented the search for the "historical" Jesus. Liberal scholars have attempted to reconstruct the life of Christ using sources other than Scripture, ending up with precious little in the process and, in so doing, undermining the faith of many. Some have come to believe that Jesus was a sage, a guru, a Jewish mystic, a magician, even a political revolutionary.

Who is this Man Jesus Christ? His identity is inseparable from the redemption of mankind. Jesus Christ is not one path among many to eternal life. He claimed to be "*the* way, *the* truth, and *the* life. No ones comes to the Father except through me" (John 14:6, emphasis added). Notice that Jesus did not claim to *have* the way, or even to *know* the way; He claimed to *be* the way. His imperialistic claims set Him apart from every other religious leader in history.

The claims clash with postmodern thinking. In a pluralistic culture, many people choose to identify Jesus as a prophet, or even a good, moral man, while refusing to acknowledge Him as the only begotten Son of God. But this logic does not hold. If He was not who He claimed to be—the Son of God, coequal with the Father—then He was deceitful, He could not be a sacrifice for sin, and He cannot even be credited with being a good moral teacher.

In order for His blood to serve as the atonement for fallen man, Jesus Christ had to be both God and man. The fact that He was, and is, fully God authorizes Him to offer Himself as a perfect sacrifice for sin. The fact that He was, and is, fully man means that, as a human, He had the right to die in our place. Jesus Christ's humanity was as genuine as His deity, thereby reconciling unholy, sinful man to a holy, sinless God.

6. The Holy Spirit Is Actively at Work in the World

Of the three Persons in the Godhead—Father, Son and Holy Spirit—the Spirit is probably the least known and understood. Yet it is the Holy Spirit, as the "executive agent" of the Godhead, who is involved with us personally, drawing us to the Father, baptizing us into Christ, filling us with power and leading us into spiritual maturity. Not only is He involved with us individually, but He is responsible for the development of the Church in this present age.

In spite of the cultural disintegration around us, the Holy Spirit is actively at work in the world today. We also recognize (as we saw in Charles Colson's comment in chapter 2) the fundamental difference between *saving grace* and *common grace*. The Holy Spirit is the agent of both. He is working to draw men to the saving knowledge of Jesus Christ, while also restraining the flood of evil that would otherwise overwhelm the world. Our current cultural crisis reflects not His lack of willingness to change the nations, but rather our unwillingness to surrender to His agenda.

7. The Kingdom of God Is Destined to Prevail over Every World System

When Communists assumed control of China in 1947, the regime expelled every foreign missionary from the nation. Many faithful believers were forced to leave, fearing that the demonic forces of Communism would destroy the work of God. To many the battle seemed lost. Yet forty years later, when China was reopened to foreign visitors, a thriving underground church was evident. The powers of Communism were no match for the rule and reign of Jesus Christ.

The term *Kingdom of God* is used throughout the Scripture to describe God's rule in the world. Just over two thousand years ago, the reign of God invaded time and history in the Person of Jesus Christ. He began His earthly ministry by proclaiming the arrival of the Kingdom. This announcement marked His inauguration— the beginning of His eternal reign on earth. God in Christ had come to man. The message of the Kingdom is also known as "the government of God," and reveals His incontestable right to command all peoples and nations according to the counsel of His own will.

But one might look at our cultural decline and wonder if God really is in control. After all—and this argument is one of the biggest impediments to faith—how could a loving God sit idly by while children die of cancer or are murdered by their schoolmates? Where is God in the midst of natural disasters that claim thousands of lives each year? Why doesn't He intervene when nation rises against nation and precious children are caught in the crossfire? The purposes of God are not immediately seen in the midst of darkness and despair, but in His sovereignty God has chosen to invest His power and authority in the hands of His people, the Church. The better question is not "Where is God?" but "Where is the Church?"

It is also important that we distinguish between the act of believing in the existence of God and surrendering to His desire to rule in every area of our lives. The same God who created the world continues to control it. He is actively working out His redemptive purposes in human history, and He longs to use the Church as the instrument of revival, restoration and reformation.

I believe we are standing on the precipice of a worldwide reformation that will transform many aspects of the Church and how we relate to contemporary culture.

Your Answer Determines Your Destiny

One of the weakest areas in contemporary Christendom, as we have seen in this chapter, is the inconsistency of our biblical worldview. Do we as Christians have the right to challenge the systems of this world that enslave fallen humanity, whether they be political, social, financial, educational or economic? This question begs for an answer! Furthermore we should ask ourselves, Does the earth belong to the Lord, and we are called to occupy it until He comes again, or does it belong to the devil, and we should therefore abandon it?

The answers to these questions, I am convinced, will determine the destiny of our families, churches, cities and nations. Our biblical worldview affects the very mission of the Church.

But the Church has been more interested in "flying away" than in changing the world. I find it tragic that Christianity is the only religion with the real power to change the planet, yet the only one without a consistent social agenda.

We cannot deny that others' view of life is changing rapidly. It is not your father's worldview. But if you are seeing the culture around you from a biblical worldview, then what do you do about it?

5

WHERE IN THE WORLD IS THE CHURCH?

The thing a man does practically believe; the thing
a man does practically lay to heart, and know for
certain, concerning his vital relations to this mysterious Universe, and his duty and destiny here . . .
that is his religion.

Thomas Carlyle

Most of the Jews deported to Babylon were
resettled along the Chebar River, a canal northeast of the city. It is
probable that they were conscripted for labor on Nebuchadnezzar's
vast building projects in the nearby city. This left the Jews free to
live in the security of their own communities, preserving some
degree of their values, customs and culture but dependent on the
Babylonians for food, shelter and protection. They were forced into
ghettos with few freedoms, limited resources and a small number
of advocates within the government. Many of the exiles abandoned
all hope for the future.

Not Daniel. He knew he could not shrink from the challenge. Although most of the Jewish exiles resigned themselves to seventy years of oppression, Daniel recognized that the only hope for his people lay in engaging and transforming the culture in which they found themselves captive. He began to position himself for societal infiltration.

Christians must reflect carefully on their relationship to a culture that has become increasingly secular, even hostile to our identity as spiritual exiles. I am convinced that the primary reason many Christians have avoided Christ's Great Commission to disciple the nations is that we have misinterpreted a number of Scriptures, like the one that warns us not to be friends with the world. An improper understanding of God's Word has rendered us socially and evangelistically impotent.

Since the Bible uses the word *world* in a variety of ways, we should not assume it is being used the same way in every context. The word *lion,* for example, is used as a symbol of both Jesus and Satan. Only by interpreting the verse in context can we properly discern the identity of the image. Another example is the word *serpent.* Lucifer slithered through the Garden of Eden in his quest to deceive Adam and Eve. Furthermore, in the teachings of Jesus serpents were used as symbols of evil (see Matthew 23:33; Mark 16:18; Luke 10:19). Yet, remarkably, a serpent was lifted up on a pole in the wilderness as a type of Christ, who was lifted up on the cross (see Numbers 21:8; John 3:14).

Once again we must interpret the image in its proper context in order to understand the symbolism.

So What Exactly Is "the World"?

As with the words *lion* or *serpent, world* can also be interpreted as a designation of evil or good. One meaning of the Greek word *kosmos* refers to the world as a hostile ethical system. While God's intention is to redeem the willing of the planet, the world system has always opposed His rule and order and will continue to war against His eternal purpose. I have listed several of the ways the word *world* can be interpreted.

A Symbol of the Created Order

Kosmos, the Greek word for *world,* is used to designate the whole of creation and, even more specifically, planet earth. Genesis 1:31 reveals that the world was created by God and that it was "very good." "[Jesus] was in the world, and the world was made through Him. . ." (John 1:10).

A Way to Identify Humanity

"God so loved the world that He gave His only begotten Son, that whoever believes in Him should not perish but have everlasting life" (John 3:16). Rightly interpreted, *the world* must be understood in this context as the whole of humanity.

A Way to Distinguish the Elect from the Non-Elect

"I do not pray for the world but for those whom You have given Me, for they are Yours" (John 17:9). Prior to Christ's coming, two worlds existed (with some exceptions), dividing Jew and Gentile. Two worlds still exist, but the division is between believers and unbelievers.

A Symbol of a Hostile Ethical System

"Do you not know that friendship with the world is enmity [hostility] with God?" (James 4:4). When we contrast this statement with the teachings of Jesus, we must conclude that this passage is referring to the world as a hostile ethical system.

In His great High Priestly prayer, Jesus prayed that believers would remain *in* the world (geographically and socially) but not *of* the world (adopting the value system hostile to Christ and His Word). Whether we love the world because the love of God is *in* us, or whether we love the world because the love of God is *not* in us, all depends on how it is that we love the world. That is not as complicated as it sounds! You simply have to interpret each use of *kosmos* in the context of the surrounding texts.

How are the righteous supposed to relate to the world? That is not an easy question, but it is one that should make you think. How does God Himself, in all His righteousness and holiness, relate to a world that has turned to either idolatry or self-indulgence? Our responsibility to relate to the world should be like God's own actions toward the world.

The world (*kosmos,* God's creation), and all who live in it, are the objects of God's redeeming love. He demonstrated His love for the world by giving His only Son. In contrast, Scripture warns us, "Do not love the world *[kosmos]* or the things in the world. If anyone loves the world, the love of the Father is not in him. For all that is in the world—the lust of the flesh, the lust of the eyes, and the pride of life—is not of the Father but is of the world. And the world is passing away, and the lust of it; but he who does the will of God abides for ever" (1 John 2:15–17).

The Myth of Separation

When secularism ascended the intellectual throne of influence in the Western world many years ago, religious ideas, values and institutions began being pushed to the fringe. More recently in America, the intellectual and cultural powers that be drew a line of separation between the secular and the sacred. Much of the Church, unfortunately, adopted this two-sphere mentality.

A lot can be said about how the Church has progressively abandoned political and social institutions and turned them over to secular humanists and pagans. Without going into great detail, let me say simply that we never abandoned anything by our lack of involvement that we did not first abandon in our thinking and in our worldview. Once you buy into a secular-versus-sacred dualism, or a two-sphere mentality, retreating into a subculture or counterculture is only a matter of time.

For America's drift toward secularism and injustice, Francis Schaeffer blamed the Christian community's failure to apply its worldview to every facet of society. "The basic problem of the Christians in this country in the past eighty years or so, in regard to society and in regard to government," he wrote, "is that they have seen things in bits and pieces instead of totals."[1]

One of the chief reasons we have seen Christianity in bits and pieces is that we have created improper distinctions between the secular and the sacred. Most Christians divide life into two spheres, thereby diminishing our responsibility and influence.

Not Dietrich Bonhoeffer, who once declared:

> There are not two realities, but only one reality, and that is the reality of God, which has become manifest in Christ in the reality of the world. . . . There are not two spheres but only the one sphere of the realization of Christ, in which the reality of God and the reality of the world are united.[2]

Unfortunately, many Christians no longer believe that all of life is religious, so they compartmentalize their faith. They have been duped into believing that prayer, worship and ministry must be separated from the "carnal" aspects of life such as work, marriage, sex, economics, education and athletics (to name just a few). They have successfully separated God from their hopes, dreams, ambitions and careers.

The enemy has deceived many Christians into believing that to be involved with "secular work"—that is, work with meaning for the here and now—is less than spiritual. This is a falsehood. As far as God is concerned, and as far as the labor itself is concerned, there is no difference between spiritual work and secular work. The difference is in the motive and outcome. I have done secular work in the pulpit, when I have labored in my own strength to accomplish a personal agenda, and I have done spiritual work in society because I did it as unto the Lord.

This Is My Father's House

"The earth is the LORD'S, and all its fullness, the world and those who dwell therein," declared the psalmist (Psalm 24:1). St. Francis of Assisi saw all of creation as his house of worship, and called on everything in the created order to join him in worship of the one true and living God—the fiery sun, the silver moon, the evening stars, planet earth, shimmering water, cool wind, lofty mountains, fruitful trees. The saint abandoned nothing to the spiritual forces of secularism. He considered everything sacred in his Father's world.

The great revivalist A. W. Tozer once wrote:

> Everything depends upon the state of our interior lives and our heart's relation to God. The man who walks with God will see and know that for him there is no strict line separating the sacred from the secular. He will acknowledge that there lies around him a world of created things that are innocent in themselves; and he will know, too, that a thousand human acts are neither good nor bad except as they may be done by good or bad men.[3]

Do you really think God limits His concerns to only those elements within the religious realm? How preposterous! If the alternating use of *kosmos* in the Scriptures seems confusing and almost contradictory, it is because dedicated Christians are almost always more isolated in their thinking than God is. He does not have a dualistic view of the world; it all belongs to Him! If the cattle on a thousand hills are His, then He certainly owns more than just the sacred ones. Jesus gave the Great Commission for us to go not just to the sacred world, but into the entire world, and disciple it.

A Crash Course in Paganism

What must it have been like for the young men brought to Nebuchadnezzar's court for training and reeducation? Daniel, an Israelite, a son of Judah, probably with some connection to the royal family of King David, had been taught the commandments from childhood. The first and foremost of those commandments was expressed like this:

> "I am the LORD your God who brought you out of the land of Egypt, out of the house of bondage. You shall have no other gods before Me. You shall not make for yourself a carved image—any likeness of anything that is in heaven above, or that is in the earth beneath. . . . You shall not bow down to them nor serve them. For I, the LORD your God, am a jealous God. . . ."
>
> Deuteronomy 5:6–9

In addition to the first commandment, a large portion of the ceremonial law was dedicated to isolating and protecting God's chosen people from the corrupting influences of the pagan cultures that surrounded them. The Law was a barrier to keep out the cultural defilement. Even more central to the ceremonial law were the prescriptions and regulations regarding atonement for sin, all of which were based on the Temple sacrifices.

Nebuchadnezzar had completely destroyed Jerusalem. The Jews had spent their lives in a setting where righteousness was measured, in part, by the degree to which they distanced themselves from the ideas and practices of idolatry. But following the third Babylonian invasion of Judah, there was no Temple, no sacrifice and, for the Jews who had been marched off to Babylon, no wall of separation.

It is interesting to note that the first commandment to worship the God of Abraham exclusively, giving no place for idolatry, was introduced with the phrase *I am the LORD your God who brought you out of the land of Egypt, out of the house of bondage.* The commandment had not changed, but the faces of their captors had. Think about it. In an unimaginable turn of events, Israel's royal seed had once again become slaves and were being trained this time in the language, art, literature and civilization of Babylon. Talk about culture shock! For someone who loved God and was dedicated to His service, it was—putting it in the mildest possible terms—a demoralizing situation. If God wanted to teach Daniel how to swim in the waters of a pagan culture, He did so by throwing him into the deep end.

Much rationalizing and compromising takes place among people who are in the process of being culturally absorbed. There is a conflict between the values they once held dear and what they seem to have to do now to get ahead—or maybe just to survive. When Daniel and his friends refused to eat the king's meat, I am sure the other young Jews had some advice for them.

"What do you guys think you're doing? You're going to get us all killed! This is no time to be self-righteous, and it's not a good idea to complain about the king's food. Can't you see God has spared our lives by bringing us here? Why would He have allowed us to be brought here if He didn't want us to eat the king's meat? Look, everyone else is eating it."

Their desire to make it in the kingdom of Babylon probably produced in them all kinds of rationalizing arguments to justify their compromises. But the pathway to dominion—which I define as "serving your way into a place of responsible influence," according to Genesis 1—is neither compromise nor inflexibility about things that do not really matter. It is knowing when to sit quietly and when to take a stand for principles. Those with only a cursory knowledge of God's Word, and who have casually followed Christ, will have a hard time figuring out the difference.

Walking the Razor's Edge

Like Daniel, his friends and all the other Jews in Babylon, we are continually faced with the subtle but dangerous pressure of living in a foreign culture that can defeat our mission, in one of two ways. On the one hand we can be so absorbed in a foreign culture that we lose our distinctive identity as Christians and the effectiveness of our witness. On the other hand we can be segregated and marginalized by the dominant culture to the degree that we lose our relevance—and, once again, our effective testimony.

We face the same three options Daniel faced: to *receive* the culture as the standard of conduct for our lives; to *reject* the culture in a callous state of indifference; or to *reform* the culture by demonstrating God's rulership (in our case, the Lordship of Christ) in every arena of life.

Dr. Richard Lovelace, in his book *The Dynamics of Spiritual Life,* studied the theological dynamics that have contributed to, or detracted from, sudden awakenings and continuous spiritual renewal throughout Church history.[4] The primary elements, or "preconditions for revival," were the awareness of God's holiness on the one hand, and a simultaneous awareness of the depth of sin in our personal lives, as well as in the community, on the other. These two realities constitute a wide gap between God and man. The secondary elements were the preaching of the Gospel—justification by faith, the indwelling of the Spirit, sanctification and the believer's authority in spiritual conflict.

After revival begins, a number of factors determine whether the move of the Spirit will become an ongoing renewal or fade away, remembered at best by a paragraph or two in a history book. Several factors determine the movement's ability to influence society. Lovelace identifies one of those factors as the tension between protective and destructive enculturation. Each is a function of how we relate to the world.

Protective enculturation is the perspective and process by which the Church erects a wall of separation to protect herself from the world. Her members are set apart as so distinct that they become irrelevant. Destructive enculturation, on the other hand, is the process of reaching out and identifying with the world in such a way that the Church is corrupted by worldly influences.

Protective Enculturation

Think of a castle set up on a hill, complete with fortifications, moat and drawbridge. It strategically overlooks the city below—the city of man. People have retreated to the castle to worship God, to fellowship with one another and to escape the corruption of the world. They have been redeemed, cleansed and filled. They have a passion for purity, righteousness and even true worship that is pleasing to God. They want to be all God wants them to be, and to maintain that high standard they have to establish rules and regulations. These principles happen to be posted at the entrance to the castle.

A lot of wonderful things go on there, but it all seems pretty strange to the people living down in the city. In the local hangouts the action on the hill is periodically a topic of conversation, as well as the subject of gross mischaracterization.

"I used to know a guy who lives up there now," says one. "He used to go fishing with some of the guys from work. He loved to fish, but since he moved up there, we haven't seen much of him."

"I heard they do some really spooky things up there," says his friend.

"Yeah? Like what?"

"Well, did you know they're not allowed to use deodorant?"

"You're kidding."

"That's right. I think it's like—those who are really religious have the fragrance of the Lord on 'em, so deodorant is for those who don't have enough faith."

"Man, that's weird! But I really liked the guy who used to fish with us. He was funny. He had a nice boat, too. Think we could get him to come back?"

"Naw. I heard he's pretty committed."

"Well, you know Joe went up there to visit last week, and he's the only other one of us with a boat. If he gets sucked in, we're fishing from the bank!"

"Whoa! You'd better have a little talk with Joe before it's too late."

The folks up in the castle really are good people and would love for all their old friends from the city of man to join them. They used to send out commando evangelists to rescue (sometimes they slip and say "capture") some people and bring them back. Once they sent out a few evangelists and never saw them again. Among those who never returned was the man with the fishing boat, who himself was captured by his old friends. That horrified the leaders, who pulled up the drawbridge and strung up some barbed wire. They went back to the old strategy of lobbing Gospel mortar shells from their tactical position down into the city, hoping some of the people would become frightened enough to escape the city, run the gauntlet and make their way up to the castle.

It is difficult, if not impossible, to express genuine care and consideration for a community while we are at the same time concentrating our efforts on keeping away from it. When isolationists hear about the problems of the Babylonians, rather than empathize with them, they are more likely to think, *Yeah, that's why we need to stay away from those people.*

This is the state of mind that drove the priest and the Levite to pass the wounded man lying in the ditch. We often describe this kind of person as "so heavenly minded he is no earthly good." They seem to have forgotten that Jesus was the most heavenly minded Man who ever lived, yet He also "went about doing good and healing" people (Acts 10:38). The modern parallel: people who major on church services as a substitute for living the Christian life seven days a week. The priest and Levite have learned to shut their eyes and hearts to Babylonians who are in need. A modern-day Good Samaritan might be considered less spiritual because of his concern for the "carnal" affairs of life rather than seeking those things that are above.

Destructive Enculturation

Culturally absorbed Christians are those whose hearts have been captivated by the lust of the flesh, the lust of the eyes and the pride of life. They love the world, but not the way God loves it. They find their source of nourishment and identity in world systems and cannot bear to forsake them. Remember Lot's wife, who loved Sodom and, against God's command, looked back longingly to it. A culturally absorbed Christian cannot be distinguished from those who identify with the spirit of the world. Unlike Daniel, the culturally absorbed Christian sits at the king's table, bows before his idols and worships at the shrine of cultural sovereignty.

This individual, though he still may make a show of being religious, has become captive to the world's value system. He has absorbed the spirit of the age and, as a result, become self-absorbed. In learning to speak the language of Babylon, he has crossed the line of scriptural principles, ignored the voice of his conscience and defiled his own soul.

Some people in the city of man came to believe in the message being preached up on the hill, but for various reasons never became committed to the castle. Many of them loved the city's convenience and culture so much that they just could not give it up.

Since you used to live down in that city, perhaps you remember the hangouts. People talk about their need to become more religious and throw in an occasional mention of their need to get back to church. Many will even tell you they are on a fast track to hell, that Jesus is their only hope and that everyone within earshot needs to become a Christian. Though what they say may be simplistic, and at times a little off theologically, they give a pretty good explanation of the Gospel. But what they say does not really affect other people. If you do not live what you believe, your words have no power to transform people's lives. That is one of the effects of being absorbed into a foreign culture. You lose your unique identity, and your witness is so watered down with fundamental compromise that it lacks the power to affect anyone.

Revivals, whether personal, regional or national, usually begin with a deep penetration into the secular and pagan world—that is, the city of man. The power of the Holy Spirit is manifested by transforming great sinners—those who seem the least likely candidates for the Kingdom of God—into dedicated and passionate Christians. Consequently the whole community sees the power of God demonstrated.

But the effectiveness of the movement to continue penetrating deeply into the world of nonbelievers is determined by its ability to avoid the pitfalls of enculturation, either protective or destructive. Some of the mainline denominations, for example, grew out of the Great Awakenings and continued for many years to effectively transform lives and culture. In the last fifty years, however, they have allowed the value system of spiritual Babylon to dominate their identity as offspring of the Kingdom. Having lost their unique Christian distinctive, their witness was silenced.

A counter example would be the birth and emergence of the Pentecostal and Holiness movements. In spite of continued zeal and dedication, many have gone the way of the Amish and lost the ability to deeply penetrate the enemy's territory.

The Qualities of a Reformer

It is easy to sit at a distance and debate the finer points of infiltrating the world. In fact, that is exactly how many Christians interact with the culture in general and worldly individuals in particular: sitting at a distance and talking about it now and then. The more difficult task is putting that love into practice and determining exactly how we relate to the world on a practical level.

Daniel's response in light of the opportunity set before him was to learn the language of Babylon so he would be capable of communicating in the tongue of his captors. In time he was able to penetrate the hardened soil of their pagan culture in an extraordinary way.

Here are seven practical pointers we can learn from Daniel about turning our captivity into an opportunity to infiltrate the culture as a witness for Christ.

1. Daniel Entered the Culture with the Outcome in View

"The chief official gave them new names. . . . But Daniel resolved not to defile himself with the royal food and wine" (Daniel 1:7–8, NIV). If you start down this road without being crystal clear about your absolute allegiance, you will gradually be absorbed and transformed into a Babylonian. In many ways Daniel assumed the appearance of a Babylonian, but he maintained the purity of his essential core values and beliefs.

No genuine Christian, regardless of individual ingenuity or charisma, can live in a post-Christian culture without periodically encountering a clash of values. If you lack Daniel's determination, or if you are waiting to see what the cost of discipleship will be, you will never be a successful infiltrator. Jesus said to count the cost on the front end.

When we moved to Scottsdale, Arizona, to establish CitiChurch International, my wife and I decided to enroll our three children in the public school system. For some time God had been dealing with Judith and me concerning the need to penetrate the culture with the Gospel. And, frankly, the proposition is easier to consider when you are not risking your very own children. In the wake of the nationwide epidemic of high school shootings, this seemed a most inappropriate time to consider removing our children from the presupposed security of a parochial school environment.

This topic became a major part of our discussion in family devotions. We examined the issue from every possible angle. The questions were not easily resolved. Months after we made the decision and the children had enrolled in school, Judith and I continued to consider our position. It is one of the most difficult decisions Christian parents have to make, and every situation is different. The fundamental question we must ask ourselves is this: Have our kids settled the issue in their own minds about who they are and whom they are going to serve?

Because of Judith's and my commitment to learning the language of Babylon, our children have had an impact on those in their public schools. Terry, our oldest son, persuaded one of his unsaved teachers to come to a dramatic production at church, and as a result she gave her life to Christ. They have been involved in changing school policies and opening up new opportunities for the Gospel to be communicated. The challenge of living for Christ in a postmodern environment has become a catalyst for their spiritual growth. In fact, our kids have penetrated the culture more deeply, and have had a more significant impact on their friends, than their parents have!

2. Daniel Chose His Battleground Carefully

Rather than allow his enemies to determine the boundaries of the battlefield, Daniel separated the negotiables from the non-negotiables. He was forced into captivity and accepted Babylonian oppression because he saw the opportunity for his God to prevail. They changed his name, and he consented because he knew who he really was. He was forced to learn the literature of Babylon, and accepted their instructions because he knew what he believed. But when they demanded that he eat the king's meat, he appealed to their better judgment. And when they required him to stop praying to Jehovah, he defied their orders. Even in his youth Daniel had the ability to distinguish between a cultural preference and a clear-cut violation of God's command.

Sometimes zealous Christians take bold, uncompromising stands on issues that are relatively insignificant. If the office party is going to be held at a restaurant that serves alcohol, and you complain that the selection discriminates against your religious preferences, you come off as weird, arrogant and self-righteous. People who major in minors do so because they are more interested in making a statement than in making a disciple. What good is it if you change all the rules to accommodate your beliefs when, in the end, everyone hates you, and what you believe as well? My friend Joseph Garlington often asks the question, "Do you want to be *right* or *reconciled?*"

Daniel knew when to take a stand and when to bite his lip and tolerate the Babylonians, simply doing what the Babylonians did. I am convinced that most Christians need to settle this simple truth in their minds once and for all. Sinners are only doing what they have always done. They are sinning. Their identity as sinners determines their actions. We cannot expect sinners to espouse the values we hold dear without a conversion experience. So don't be outraged when they confirm their identity by sinning. The more important issue is: Are *you* living up to *your* identity as a disciple of Jesus Christ?

Throughout his career, in which he rose to be prime minister of the Assyrian empire, Daniel had to endure a lot that was repugnant to his Jewish sensibilities. But when it came to a simple thing like his three-times-daily prayers, he would not compromise, though it meant going to the lions' den. He would not even shut the window to pray in secret, when he probably knew they were just waiting to catch him.

It takes wisdom, discernment and divine guidance to figure out when to dig in and take a stand and when to fall back and fight another day. As I said earlier, those who have only a cursory knowledge of God's Word and who have followed Christ only casually will have a hard time determining where to draw that line.

3. Daniel Was Not Afraid to Challenge the Status Quo

"Daniel resolved not to defile himself with the royal food and wine, and he asked the chief official for permission not to defile himself this way" (Daniel 1:8, NIV). The commander feared that if Daniel and his friends were not as healthy as the other youths, and it was found out that his food ration had been changed over the issue of Jewish religious principle, Nebuchadnezzar would literally have his head. Daniel responded, "Please test your servants for ten days. . . . Then let our countenance be examined before you, and the countenance of the young men who eat the portion of the king's delicacies; and as you see fit, so deal with your servants" (Daniel 1:12–13).

Not only did Daniel and his friends look healthier, but they also excelled in every area, including in spiritual activities such as interpreting visions and dreams.

At the end of three years, the king examined the four young men. "In all matters of wisdom and understanding about which the king examined them, he found them ten times better than all the magicians and astrologers who were in all his realm" (Daniel 1:20). Daniel did not use his religious preferences as an excuse for a lack of excellence. Rather, these preferences were the reason the Hebrews were determined to be the best—even better at Babylonian living than the Babylonians!

Too many times we pray for God to raise up Christians to places of influence by His power simply because they are Christians. Those who ignore the opportunity to prepare, and then look to God as a shortcut to promotion and influence, do not glorify Him.

4. Daniel Exemplified Sincere Spirituality

Daniel was not just religious; he was a truly spiritual man who sought God through every stage of his life.

The king had been tormented by a recurring dream, and threatened to kill all his counselors if they did not interpret it. The wise men and conjurers assured the king, "Sure, we'll interpret your dream. Tell us what it is." But the king knew those advisers too well, and how easily they could simply make something up. He also knew they were pleasers who only said what he wanted to hear. So Nebuchadnezzar, disturbed by the dream, resolved to find someone with genuine spirituality. He demanded that the wise men also tell him the dream. It was his test for authentic spiritual insight.

Only Daniel was able to reveal the dream in detail and interpret it. He told the king straightforwardly that his dream foretold God's judgment against him.

The world is looking for people with a genuine relationship with God. They are turned off by anything they perceive as pretense. The paradox of isolation is this: Those who have moved into the castle on the hill so they can be really close to God find themselves, over time, losing what they separated themselves to obtain. If you never interact with people and situations in which you become a witness for Christ, your spiritual life diminishes. It does not matter if you are in the Oval Office or in prison; whether you are boldly preaching the Gospel or serving needy people. If you never personally confront the darkness with the light of Christ, then your heart will grow cold.

There is also a deceptive element of religious isolation. Most castles post lists of rules and regulations that have developed over time. Following them constitutes holiness. But the deception is, you can follow all the rules but be backsliding in your heart. Those who have lived in the castle for a while have developed a lifestyle around the regulations. Consequently, following the rules is no longer a spiritual challenge; it is a habit. This is precisely what happened to the Pharisees. Eventually the characteristics of internal righteousness such as love, compassion, service and faith are replaced by pride, self-righteousness and actual contempt for people in the city of man.

5. Daniel Saw Himself as an Instrument of the Sovereign God

God puts people in positions of power and influence. It happens at appointed times for a particular purpose. The problem is, when these people "arrive," they can become territorial, compromising in order to maintain what they have achieved. They are not willing to risk their position or their relationships to take a stand for Christ.

The lives and actions of Daniel and his friends show dramatically that in their successes, they remained surrendered to God. Daniel went from the office of prime minister to the lions' den. Shadrach, Meshach and Abednego, high-ranking public officials, faced the fiery furnace rather than bow before the statue of Nebuchadnezzar.

To be an effective infiltrator you have to be willing to put it all on the line when the situation calls for it.

6. Daniel and His Friends Positioned Themselves for Greatness, Even at Personal Risk

God orchestrated bad circumstances for His greatest glory. The results were seen in the aftermath of the fiery furnace and the lions' den. After Daniel's three friends were delivered from the furnace, Nebuchadnezzar exclaimed:

> "Blessed be the God of Shadrach, Meshach, and Abed-Nego, who sent His Angel and delivered His servants who trusted in Him, and they have frustrated the king's word, and yielded their bodies, that they should not serve nor worship any god except their own God! Therefore I make a decree that any people, nation, or language which speaks anything amiss against the God of Shadrach, Meshach, and Abed-Nego shall be cut in pieces, and their houses shall be made an ash heap; because there is no other God who can deliver like this."
> Daniel 3:28–29

And the three Hebrew men were promoted yet again.

After King Darius had Daniel thrown into the lions' den, he arose at dawn and hurried to the den, to find that Daniel's God had preserved him. The king gave an order to extract revenge on those who had set up the man of God. He also wrote a letter that was sent out to all people in every nation. This is what he said:

> "I make a decree that in every dominion of my kingdom men must tremble and fear before the God of Daniel. For He is the living God, and steadfast forever; His kingdom is the one which shall not be destroyed, and His dominion shall endure to the end. He delivers and rescues, and He works signs and wonders in heaven and on earth, who has delivered Daniel from the power of the lions."
>
> Daniel 6:26–27

And Daniel himself? Scripture says he "prospered" (verse 28). I believe Daniel positioned himself strategically to challenge the Babylonian culture and reveal the power of the One he served.

7. Daniel Refused to Play the Humanistic Advancement Game

Throughout the seventy years of his captivity, Daniel saw some significant changes in Babylon, some for the better, others for the worse. But through it all he remained faithful to the God of Israel. Daniel survived, by the grace of God, "through all the plots and intrigues that regularly existed in Oriental courts; through all the jealousy and envy that could only be expected toward a foreign captive in high office; through a series of four rapid successions of Babylonian kings, two of which had suffered assassination; and through the fall of Babylon itself to the genius of Cyrus, the Medeo-Persian."[5]

God used these young princes of Judah to infiltrate and influence a pagan culture in a way that is unprecedented in history. The biblical account does not suggest that these young Hebrews were plotting the overthrow of Babylonian religious tradition. They were simply full of character, faithful and dedicated to what they believed. And they took the Kingdom of God to the highest levels in the land of the enemy.

6

MINDING YOUR OWN BUSINESS

Fear gripped the hearts of the soothsayers.
Their carefully constructed masks of confidence began to crack.

Since the days of Nimrod, the dark arts had flourished in Babylon. Many cultures in the ancient world practiced occultism, but the Babylonians distinguished themselves by institutionalizing the magic arts as part of their government (see Daniel 2:2). They were particularly known throughout the world for their reliance on astrology. By charting the courses of the stars and the positions of the planets, they repeatedly attempted to predict the outcome of social and political events in the kingdom. It was a sham. Their deception knew no boundaries, as the magicians, astrologers and sorcerers lied to the nation and even to the king.

But this time Nebuchadnezzar had changed his tactics. Rather than ask for the interpretation of his dream (as we saw in the last chapter), he demanded that they reveal the dream itself. There was no way they could deceive him this time. The sorcerers stalled. In one last-ditch effort, they attempted to deceive the king into revealing his dream so they could fabricate an interpretation. But Nebuchadnezzar refused to wait another day. When the soothsayers finally conceded defeat, he called for their immediate execution.

Hearing the screams of dying men in the inner sanctum of the palace, Daniel demanded an explanation from his teachers. None was given. But when the captain of the king's guard came to murder the princes of Judah, Daniel could contain himself no longer. In one decisive moment, he stepped over the threshold of destiny. No longer could he remain an impassive observer of Babylonian custom and culture. It was time to get involved. Their business became his business. He would reveal and interpret the dream.

Crossing the Line of Indifference

When some members of Chapel Hill Harvester Church first drove into the parking lot of the Bankhead Courts Public Housing Project, the task before them appeared daunting. This housing community had been forsaken by the city of Atlanta and overtaken by drug dealers, prostitutes and gang members. The local residents were afraid to venture out at night for fear of random gunfire, and drug dealers ruled the streets, brazenly selling crack without fear of incarceration. Police records reveal that officers were called to the apartment complex more than ten times each day. The Atlanta Housing Authority had written to a hundred churches asking for help, without a single response. A couple of local pastors finally mustered up the courage to hold a nightly prayer vigil, until they were frightened out of the neighborhood by gunfire.

In the media Bankhead Courts became a symbol of everything wrong with public housing and the catastrophic mix of poverty and drugs. When Southern Bell temporarily suspended repair service and the U.S. Postal Service halted mail delivery, Bishop Earl Paulk decided something had to be done. Rising to the pulpit one Sunday morning, he issued a challenge to his twelve thousand parishioners to "adopt" Bankhead Courts.

Patty Battle responded to the challenge.[1] With the approval of the mayor's office and the appreciation of the residents' association committee, Patty organized members of the church and went to work. At first they were met with suspicion and hostility. Many questions needed to be answered in order for the residents to begin the process of building trust. Was this just a public relations opportunity for the church, or did the parishioners really care? Was this going to be another holiday hit-and-run, or was this church in the battle for the long haul?

It took one long year to gain the residents' trust. Eventually the church turned the tide of anger, addiction and poverty through a host of social programs, including a family day, a monthly birthday club, a weight-lifting program, Boy Scouts, Girls Clubs and programs designed to bolster the self-image and practical skills of the residents. Equally important, they changed the spiritual atmosphere of the housing project through Bible studies, prayer meetings and by ministering to the spiritual needs of those who were hurting.

Initially the work at Bankhead was considered a missionary endeavor. Before long, however, members of the church began to develop deep and meaningful relationships with the occupants of the housing project. The racial tensions began to melt away as the community members realized the church was not there for publicity but as a genuine act of love and kindness.

In his autobiographical account *One Blood,* Bishop Paulk writes:

> When our church first adopted the Bankhead Courts Public Housing Project, it was a real challenge to our white members. Since we had a relatively small number of black members at the time, the first volunteers for the work in the all-black Bankhead Courts were white. Many of them provided tutoring assistance to students from the development, and others conducted literacy programs, scouting programs, recreational programs, and art classes. As our church became more integrated, our black members also volunteered to go into this

community where there were great needs. This only took place, how-ever, because our people had a heartfelt conviction that this was a mission calling for their church. That is why they became involved.[2]

More than a decade has passed since the members of Chapel Hill Harvester Church first put their theology into action. Since that time they have assisted and forever changed the lives of the 1,700 residents who had been forsaken by the social agencies of Atlanta. The crime rate has decreased, drugs are no longer sold in public and the children feel safe to play in the neighborhood. Eventually the church was given the responsibility of running the community center. Refusing to rest on the laurels of their past accomplishments, Chapel Hill Harvester Church, under the prophetic leadership of Bishop Earl Paulk, has continued to demonstrate the Gospel of the Kingdom by ministering to the spiritual and social needs of this community.

Why is the Church called to be involved in the social structures of society? In his book *Christianity and the Social Order*, William Temple, the late Archbishop of Canterbury, pointed out the fundamental reason. Christianity, he wrote, is the most materialistic religion on earth in that it is the only religion capable of integrating with integrity the material world and the spiritual realm.[3] Christians are the only ones in society who have the basis from which to respond to both spiritual and social concerns. Ray Bakke observes, "We Christians are the only people who can truly discuss the salvation of men's souls and the rebuilding of city sewer systems in the same sentence."[4]

Relevant Christians in a Changing World

What does it mean to serve as a relevant Christian in contemporary society? In his 1963 Earl Lectures at Harvard Divinity School, noted liberal theologian Paul Tillich brilliantly framed the philosophical answer to the question:

> What is relevance? Everyone knows such a word in the usual sense, but we must ask more exactly for its meaning in the context of our problem. In that context, "relevant" means that the Christian

message answers the existential questions of humanity today. "Irrelevant" means that it does not answer those questions. By "existential" questions I refer to those which concern the whole of human existence: not only knowing, but also feeling and willing—all sides of our being as they come together in the center of the personality.[5]

Tillich gave further definition to the importance of connecting to the culture by articulating a few of the questions:

> What does it mean to be a human being in a world full of evil in body and mind, in individual and society? Where do I get the courage to live? How can I have hope? And for what? How can I overcome the conflicts that torture me inwardly? Where can I find an ultimate concern that overcomes my emptiness and has the power to transform? These are existential questions. They could also be called passionate quests for a meaningful life. Is Christian preaching, as it is done today, able to answer these questions and longings for a healing message?[6]

Since I am writing in this book, in part, to leaders on every level, I want to broaden Paul Tillich's premise considerably. Christian preaching, in and of itself, will never change the culture. The mandate to infiltrate and transform the world in which we live is the responsibility of every individual Christian. Whether your mission is touching multitudes or individuals, changing communities or diapers, planning cities or evening meals, redeeming nations or grocery coupons, reforming social structures or structuring your child's homework, you need to be relevant to those you are attempting to lead. Whether you are leading Cub Scouts or a congregation, you need to follow the pattern of Jesus and engage the culture for the purpose of transformation.

In His brief three-and-a-half-year ministry, Jesus successfully extended both arms of salvation to those who were lost, disenfranchised and without hope in Israel. Through compassionate interaction He extended the opportunity for them to receive eternal life, while also reaching out to feed the hungry, heal the sick and encourage the outcast.

Occasionally Christian groups set out to serve people and the community with the sole purpose of making a statement or making converts. If conversions do not start happening pretty quickly, they abandon the effort because it is not "bearing fruit." It is worth noting that Jesus ministered to the physical needs of those who had little or no means of supporting His ministry, nor did they have great power and influence. He had no expectation of return, and there often seemed to be nothing strategic about what He did. Jesus served people physically and spiritually simply because He loved them.

Has it ever occurred to you that serving others out of compassion, without expecting anything in return, is an end in itself?

In His very first message Jesus declared:

> "The Spirit of the LORD is upon Me, because He has anointed Me to preach the gospel to the poor. He has sent Me to heal the brokenhearted, to preach deliverance to the captives and recovering of sight to the blind, to set at liberty those who are oppressed, to preach the acceptable year of the Lord."
>
> Luke 4:18–19

Not only did Jesus preach the redemption message of the Law and the prophets, but He brought insight into God's intention for the well-being of every man and woman—spirit, soul and body. Jesus revolutionized the way God was being "served" in His generation. The New Testament Church, following Jesus' pattern, preached the Gospel, cared for widows and orphans, raised relief funds for a national tragedy and gave to the poor.

Sphere Sovereignty

Abraham Kuyper was one of the most remarkable men in the history of Reformed Christianity. In addition to serving as the prime minister of the Netherlands from 1901–1905, Kuyper was a statesman, pastor, theologian, journalist, philosopher and the founder of the Free University of Amsterdam in 1880. He has been called the greatest evangelical thinker since Jonathan Edwards, writing extensively and lecturing on the importance of reforming the social structures of society.

Kuyper was convinced that the sovereignty of God and the Lordship of Jesus Christ governed the affairs of history. He believed that Christ was sent to redeem every aspect of society, and that the Church is left with the responsibility to complete what He initiated. In Kuyper's brilliant writings on *Common Grace,* he challenged Christians to reject every view that would confine God's work to the small sector we might label church life.

In his inaugural address at the Free University on October 20, 1880, Kuyper challenged the withdrawal of the Church from the public sector by declaring, "There is not one square inch in the whole domain of our human existence over which Christ, who is Sovereign over all, does not cry: 'Mine!'"[7] This lecture formed the basis for Kuyper's teaching on "sphere sovereignty," when he divided "sovereignty in the individual social spheres" into seven basic areas—state government, family, religion, business vocation, education, science and the arts. He then divided these seven areas into two different spheres. In consideration of almighty God's sovereign right to rule the nations, Kuyper stated:

> The sovereignty of God, in its descent upon men, separates into two spheres. On the one hand, the mechanical sphere of State authority, and on the other hand the organic sphere of the authority of the social circles. And in both these spheres the inherent authority is sovereign, that is to say, it has above itself nothing but God.[8]

It is important for us to distinguish between the two spheres of authority Kuyper described, as over against the two spheres—the sacred and the secular—that we addressed in chapter 5. Kuyper divided these arenas in order to illustrate the corresponding responsibility that man has to the sovereignty of God. He did not distinguish between the sacred and the secular, but saw the world as the stage on which the drama of God's supreme will is displayed.

I want to comment briefly on each of the seven realms of sovereignty because they are the channels through which the value system of the Western world is expressed. My purpose is not to provide an academic blueprint for cultural reclamation, but rather to awaken you to the driving purpose behind our need to learn the language of Babylon. If common grace has a target in this generation, then these seven realms are of the highest consideration. As you read about each realm, please remember that it takes both common grace and saving grace to preserve, restore and reform a culture or nation.

The First Sphere

Kuyper described, first of all, "the mechanical sphere of State authority." Let me offer a historical example of a man active in this sphere.

William Wilberforce, a Member of Parliament for 45 years, was one of Britain's great social reformers. Wilberforce was converted to Christ after an intense intellectual struggle a few years before he became a Member of Parliament. If he became a Christian, he felt, he would have to abandon his political aspirations and give up his circle of friends. He wanted both.

At a crucial time in that conflict, he sought the counsel of former slave trader John Newton, who was then an Anglican priest and the author of many hymns, including "Amazing Grace." In the words of biographer John Pollock, Newton "urged him not to cut himself out from his present circles or to retire from public life." Two years later Newton wrote to him, "It is hoped and believed that the Lord has raised you up for the good of His church and for the good of the nation."

Wilberforce took Newton's advice and stayed in politics, even though at that time in history "most evangelicals shunned public life as worldly."[9] He became the most influential figure in the movement resulting in the abolition of slavery in Britain.

Even though the answer to our current cultural crisis does not lie in political redemption, we desperately need men and women of godly character in this dark hour to serve their nations. "Righteousness exalts a nation, but sin is a reproach to any people" (Proverbs 14:34). But many Christians today, like Wilberforce, struggle with the idea of combining commitment to God with their involvement in world systems.

The Second Sphere

The second sphere of the sovereignty of God, "the organic sphere of the authority of the social circles," was divided by Kuyper into six remaining areas, which in the balance of this chapter I want to develop and elaborate on.

Our Mission in the Family

In an attempt to uncover Americans' shifting social mores, George Gallup Jr. wrote a book titled *Forecast 2000*.[10] In a disturbing chapter on "The Faltering Family," Gallup discussed a number of surveys highlighting key areas over which the American family needs to be alert. He identified four issues that have contributed to the deterioration of family values: alternative lifestyles, sexual morality, economic concerns and grassroots feminist philosophy.

One would have to be morally blind to miss the relational fragmentation we see around us in society. We are living in a war zone. The casualty rate is mounting as the nuclear family continues to be devalued by humanistic influences operating through our entertainment industry. Promoting distorted male-female relationships and unnatural family situations, sitcom television, certain forms of pop music, even the media have created a demonic synergy working to deconstruct God's original intention for the family.

The family unit was formed as the basic building block of every other institution that exists under the government of heaven. God wants to see His heart and nature expressed through every relationship that exists on the earth. So the blueprint for every social relationship, from the beginning of creation, is the pattern for the family. The principles that govern our interpersonal relationships all have their roots in the family structure.

The enemy has so distorted God's plan for society that even the most conservative-minded people are tempted to modify the blueprint. But as different as God's plan may seem, it is the only pattern that will bring the results men and women desire. Every other plan will eventually lead to disorder and loss. No other substitute plan or modification will ever bring righteousness, peace and joy. The so-called alternative lifestyles that we see around us will eventually lead to poverty of soul and to death.

Our Mission in the Church

Faced with a deteriorating culture and her own declining influence, the Church cannot ignore the warning signs that threaten her existence. Reformation is needed not only among the nations, but in the soul of the Church. Clinging to powerless traditions, we have allowed ourselves to become fixated on nonessentials. When we spend more time debating the importance of proper platform attire than we spend seeking strategies for the transformation of our nation, we have become sidetracked and ineffective.

The Church is desperately in need of a reawakening of basic scriptural doctrine. Far too many Christians are biblically illiterate and spiritually bankrupt, yet we continue with business as usual. In the face of the greatest spiritual battle of history, we have allowed the prophetic impetus of the Church to be replaced by sophistication, style and consumer-oriented Christianity. Once again, at the outset of the twenty-first century, we need to make room for the awakening of apostolic and prophetic leaders who are gifted to "know what Israel ought to do." We need the present-day company of the sons of Issachar to give purpose and direction to the Church during this significant hour of transition.

The Church was designed by God to be a prophetic influence on every other sphere under the government of heaven. Although the Church (the corporate Body of Christ, not the individual) was not empowered to replace the state or even to run the affairs of state, she *is* called to influence the state to establish policies in keeping with the Word of God. Likewise the Church has no authority to dictate personal preferences to the family, or even the culture, that are not in keeping with the written absolutes of God's Word. The Church is called to influence the system of Babylon for the sake of righteousness.

Established by Jesus Christ, the Church was designed to act as salt and light in the world. As salt we preserve society from spiritual and social decay; as light we shine the light of truth to every person who lives in darkness. Ray Bakke observes, "Remember, you are never more like God than when you are living in relationships with God's people and working in partnerships for the re-creation and redemption of God's world."[11]

Our Mission in Business and Industry

Max Weber, one of the founding fathers of modern sociology, traced the origins of the work ethic. His research and study of economic behavior among Europeans led him to conclude that there was something about Protestantism that encouraged hard work and thrift. In those countries in which Protestantism dominated, he noticed that people seemed more industrious, thrifty and consequently more affluent. Weber believed that the origins of this diligence and affluence could be traced to Calvinistic theology. He also observed that the world center for capitalism—which he identified as Geneva, Switzerland—was the same city where John Calvin led his movement for religious reform in the 1550s.

Protestantism promoted a new attitude toward Christian vocation. The Catholicism of the Middle Ages urged people who wanted to serve God to leave their worldly vocations and live in convents and monasteries. But the Reformers, particularly Calvin, argued that Christians did not need to be separated from the business of worldly economics in order to render Christian service. The reformers believed that Christ could be served with total commitment in ordinary vocations. Bakers, carpenters, farmers and artisans could all serve God in their respective activities if they were able to view their work as a primary means of serving God. Ordinary economic production could be godly if the products testify to the faith of their producers.

In recent years I have discovered that ministry happens both inside and outside the local church. For too long churches have reduced ministry down to the level of singing in the choir, teaching a Sunday school class or doing hospital visitation. As a result of this limited perspective, we have excluded many members in the Body of Christ from fulfilling ministries in the marketplace.

When you awaken on Monday morning and head out for your office, you may not be on your way to preach a revival, but you are entering the greatest harvest field in the world today—what has become the Babylonian system of commerce. Your career is the broadest platform you will ever have to communicate the grace and faithfulness of God. Even in a work environment that does not allow for personal witness, you can share the evidence of God through your creativity, integrity and faithfulness.

A recent study indicates that no church can create enough meaningful jobs for all its members to serve in that setting. In fact, only a third of the membership of a local church can be given a significant job within the supportive structure of the church. On a national basis that adds up to tens of millions of Christians. So if we believe that "serving the Lord" means working within the infrastructure of the local church, two-thirds of us are doomed to frustration and disappointment.

Let me ask you three simple questions:

- Is your company in need of genuine ministry?
- Do your co-workers struggle with the purpose and meaning of their careers?
- Are you working with people who are sick, depressed, tormented, confused, hopeless and estranged from God?

If the answer to any of these questions is yes, then you have been given the greatest opportunity possible to minister! In today's competitive marketplace, most organizations require the wisdom of God in order to survive, let alone thrive. They are in need of a modern-day "Daniel Company" committed to revolutionizing the Babylonian marketplace. Are you available?

Our Mission in the Educational System

One of the primary areas of influence in any nation is the education system. This one institution provides the opportunity to shape the hearts and minds of an entire generation. Those who set the educational agenda for a nation will control the future of succeeding generations. Knowledge is power. To keep people ignorant is to control their futures and their ultimate destiny. The Old Testament prophet Hosea described it like this: "[God's] people are destroyed for lack of knowledge" (Hosea 4:6). God's reaction to universal ignorance of divine truth is ultimately to fill the earth "with the knowledge of the glory of the LORD, as the waters cover the sea" (Habakkuk 2:14).

Martin Luther argued for the Bible to be the cornerstone of a child's education:

> I am much afraid that Schools will prove to be wide gates to hell unless they diligently labor in explaining the Holy Scriptures, engraving them in the hearts of youth. I advise no one to place his child where the Scriptures do not reign paramount. Every institution in which men are not constantly occupied with the Word of God must become corrupt.

Luther's words have proven prophetically accurate. When the existence of God is eradicated from the minds of a generation, we are destined to reap the corrupt fruit of rejection and devastation. Just one generation after moral relativism became the standard of our nation, most young people today cannot distinguish between right and wrong, between morality and immorality, between normalcy and abnormalcy. The standard by which all men and women are to be judged has been rejected, leaving us without the ability to discern what is acceptable to God. Like Israel during the period of the judges, every man—or, in this case, every child—does what is right in his own eyes.

Our Mission in the Scientific Community

Do you ever wonder why secular prophets seem far more concerned about the proper stewardship of our natural resources than most Christians? Why should this be so, when the earth and all it contains belongs to the Lord (see Psalm 24:1)? Through the divine commission given to Adam, God entrusted this resource to man to manage wisely, and to use its abundance to meet the needs of others. This commission, which has come to be known as the dominion mandate, makes us accountable to God as both producers and consumers of this treasure. In order to steward the resources of planet earth properly, Christians in every nation must face and address the ecological concerns of our time. But once again the

Church has hopped onto the last float of a cultural parade being led by secular prophets, poets and musicians.

John Maddox, editor of *Nature,* the world's most prestigious science journal, wrote in the March 17, 1994, issue: "Very soon the practice of religion must be regarded as anti-science." These words would probably be as devastating to many of the early scientists as they are to their contemporary colleagues, especially because the foundation for the modern scientific revolution was laid by Bible-believing Christians like Copernicus, Sir Isaac Newton and Carl Linnaeus. These men were committed to scientific discovery because of their belief in the orderly arrangement of the universe.

The conviction that God is structured, orderly and rational provides a basis for our understanding of the structured, orderly, rational nature of the universe. Our belief in the personal Designer of the universe should position us at the forefront of the scientific community. Rather than waste precious years of research attempting to deny the signs of orderly arrangement, Christian scientists can settle the issue and can move beyond the debate into searching for the answers to our current crises.

Our Mission in the Arts

Have you grown tired of seeing the same old religious paintings captioned by Bible verses and religious clichés? Have you ever decided that a simple sunset would be far superior to the average Christian painter? Is there actually a "Christian" style of painting? And what exactly is the difference between a Christian artistic work and a secular one? Is there any such thing as a secular sunset?

A genuine sense of creativity should be expressed in everything we do, whether sacred or secular, whether painting a sunset or a family portrait. After all, we were made in the image of the supreme Creator of the universe. It was God who formed the silvery beauty of the moon, the evening glory of a desert sunset, the majestic Matterhorn, the turquoise of the Caribbean. When God created the world, He cared enough to make it beautiful. He invested His creativity along with His care in forming everything in the created order. And in His satisfaction He surveyed all the work of His hands and contentedly declared it good.

Beginning in the first chapter of Genesis, the biblical record reveals painting, sculpting, music, architecture, crafts, poetry, psalms and drama as evidence of the creative handiwork of God. We need a new generation of artists who understand that it is possible to be a Christian without painting religious scenes and writing indifferent fiction.

In one of his letters, C. S. Lewis, the relentless scholar, wrote, "I do most thoroughly agree with what you say about Art and Literature. To my mind they can only be healthy when they are either (a) admittedly aiming at nothing but innocent recreation or (b) definitely the handmaids of religious or at least moral truth."[12] Those who attempt evangelism through art as their only mission usually end up subjecting their creativity to their mission. As a result, both their art and their message are trivialized.

Perhaps the most notable artist in history was Bezaleel, a righteous man who cut and set stones, carved wood and worked in gold, silver and brass. Since God did not want to be worshiped in the same manner as pagan deities, Bezaleel was called by the Lord to work on the Tabernacle. The Scripture identifies him as the first Spirit-filled man who was gifted, skilled and able to teach all kinds of craftsmanship. Repeatedly we are told of the result of the inspiration of the Spirit in his life in "all manner of workmanship" (Exodus 35:31). To be spiritually inspired is to create.

Bezaleel's art was the sacred place where a human being met the *shekinah* glory of God. His art was not just inspired; it was inhabited by the sovereign Creator. His art was prophetic, in that it pointed to the drama of redemption. The bronze altar constructed for sacrifices, for example, represented the substitutionary death of Christ, our sinless sacrifice. The bronze laver, crafted for the washing of the priests, prophetically directs us to the cleansing of our own sin through the atoning work of Christ. Bezaleel fashioned a golden lampstand symbolizing Christ as the light of the world. The table of bread prophetically acknowledged Christ as the Bread of Life. The altar of incense represented God's Son, who lived His life in perfect obedience, as a beautiful fragrance to the Father. Each of these objects of worship, housed in the Tabernacle of Moses in the wilderness of Sinai, was constructed under the creative oversight of this man who was "filled . . . with the Spirit of God" (verse 31).

Bezaleel's counterpart in the building of the Temple, Hiram (1 Kings 7; 2 Chronicles 2), appears to be an unrighteous craftsman who also created art by drinking of common grace. Although he and his men were brought up in a culture that worshiped Ashtoreth, the goddess of lust and war, God chose them as artisans because they were skilled in carpentry. Almighty God revels in the creation of art—even, amazingly, when the vessel's foolish heart is darkened. Hiram shows us that art for art's sake, absent of evangelistic underpinnings, can and does glorify God if created in excellence.

When considering the relationship between man and art, C. S. Lewis stated:

> The first demand any work of art makes upon us is surrender. Look. Listen. Receive. Get yourself out of the way. There is no good asking first whether the work before you deserves such a surrender, for until you have surrendered, you cannot possibly find out. When a culture loses the art of surrender to God, the craftsmanship of art is soon to follow.[13]

Standing on Arbot Street in the drizzling rain, surrounded by brightly decorated vendors' booths set against the gray backdrop of the drab shops, my heart ached deep within my chest. On this miserable day in Moscow, these Russian shopkeepers were selling the artwork from their sacred temples and synagogues along with their cheap souvenirs.

This scene was being played out shortly after Communism fell, and the signs of capitalism were evident all around. While most of the paintings and icons were cheap imitations designed to fool the overzealous Western shopper, a few were, in fact, genuine.

Not too far down the street, through the main square, Russians were lining up to see an exhibit of German art treasures that had been stolen by the Red Army during World War II. These priceless artifacts were on display for the first time in more than forty years. What a study in contrasts as, back on Arbot Street, these people readily sold what they could not afford to sell!

Our Mission in the Entertainment Industry

"Give me the making of the songs of a nation," said eighteenth-century Scottish political thinker Andrew Fletcher, "and I care not who writes its laws." Who can dispute the influence of music on every generation? The artists with the greatest exposure, influence and earning potential are singers and musicians. Few children can name the great Renaissance painters, but they can readily describe the favorite adult beverage preferred by one of their music idols.

The Church has vacillated from one extreme to the other when it comes to the art form of music. To believe the message of certain fundamentalist preachers would be to resign yourself to eternal damnation for enjoying the lyrics of "easy-listening" music while riding in an elevator. On the other hand, there are people who call themselves Christians who do not object if the minds of young people are filled with violent lyrics describing every lewd act imaginable. We must find the balance between these two extremes.

There is nothing intrinsically evil about pop music, as long as it does not violate the biblical principles of purity, faithfulness and morality. The tender poems written to me by my wife contain just as much spiritual content as most of my theological writings . . . which either says something profound about the beauty of her poetry or about the drivel that I call literature! We need writers, musicians and artists in every genre of their respective fields declaring and revealing the glory of God.

Growing up in a religious environment, I was often condemned for reading secular novels. This religious imposition had a limiting effect on my education and recreation. It was only later in life that I discovered the great classics, and my worldview was expanded. As I sorted through the vain philosophies of atheists, agnostics and deists, my love for the simplicity of God's truth intensified. Through a lifetime of study and cultural observation, I am beginning to learn the language of Babylon.

Our postmodern culture elevates feelings over logic, emotions over understanding. The entertainment industry has followed suit. Most people attend movies, concerts and art galleries not to be stimulated intellectually or creatively, but in order to feel better.

Consequently they value what they feel over what they have become. While there is nothing wrong with enjoying the emotional experience—fear, delight, suspense—associated with every medium of entertainment, art is meant to communicate value and purpose to man. I believe the Church has the ability to minister in both realms—to the spiritual and intellectual dimensions of man.

Our Mission in the Media

When watching the local news or even a national broadcast, one cannot help (like Pontius Pilate) but ask the question, "What is truth?" Too many television programs synthesize fact and fiction. Agent Joe Friday of *Dragnet* would be lost in today's world. No longer do broadcasters report "just the facts, ma'am," but they skillfully blend their opinions and perspectives into the account. The Christian media do not seem to do much better. They report the news through their own doctrinal and philosophical biases, leaving us with their impressions rather than an objective account. Babylon corrupts righteousness and truth in an attempt to govern the minds of its citizens.

Our Mission in the Athletic Industry

The first Super Bowl of the new millennium was one of the greatest in the history of football, even though both teams appeared unlikely candidates just a few weeks earlier. What made this action-packed game even more exciting was the occasional crowd shot focusing in on the wives of the opposing quarterbacks, who were interceding fervently for their husbands to win!

Although Christians have not done historically well in coliseums, they are quickly taking their place as dominant figures in the athletic industry. None too soon! Plagued by greed, drug abuse and violence, the athletic community is in need of spiritual and moral revolution. When professional athletes can arrogantly say, "I refuse to be a role model for the youth of this nation," society should respond, "Then vacate the stadiums and arenas that are funded by taxpayer dollars." Lead, follow or get out of the way.

Thinking Biblically About Secular Issues

Little has changed since Abraham Kuyper gave his historic speech at the Free University of Amsterdam. The seven realms of authority he laid out still represent the battleground today. We will either win the culture war or lose to the forces of secular humanism, based on our responses to these issues. Although each of these realms holds the ability to influence the thoughts and actions of an entire populace, only the Church has the power to influence it for the sake of righteousness. Not only do we need Christian witness in these seven spheres, but we must apply the appropriate biblical principles needed to sanctify the sphere itself.

If the meek shall inherit the earth, are we minding our own business?

7

THE CHARACTER OF THE KINGDOM

Man is a moral creature, created in God's image, and we have certain absolute moral obligations toward all men.

Norman Geisler

Sphere sovereignty. I can think of no better model for spiritual and social reformation than the one given by Abraham Kuyper in the late nineteenth century. It is just as relevant now as it was then.

But before we launch a holy war against the forces of secular humanism and spiritual syncretism that are entrenched in contemporary culture, we need to consider the overarching purpose of God's Kingdom. Unless we understand the character of the Kingdom and the nature of our mission in the world, we run the risk of striking out in the wrong direction with the wrong agenda and in the wrong spirit.

A biblical comprehension of the right of the Christian to reform the culture is founded on the dynamic rule of God in a world that He governs, nation by nation, through the stewardship ministries of the Church. All history must be interpreted through the providential development of the Kingdom of God on earth. History is, in fact, *His* story. As the purpose of God prevails in the midst of each generation, His ever-increasing Kingdom is made manifest as the objective and directive of history.

Before discussing the expanding influence of the rule of Christ into every area of life, let's consider the nature and character of the Kingdom of God as it was revealed in the life and ministry of Daniel.

Kingdom Captives

The Jewish perception of the Kingdom had its root in the exile of Judah. After seventy years of captivity, a remnant under the direction of another cultural infiltrator, Nehemiah, returned from Babylon to rebuild the walls of Jerusalem and restore the city. Such a return from captivity was, with the exception of the Exodus from Egypt, unprecedented in history. It is a most improbable and astounding miracle, one that would never have taken place without God's intervention. It happened just as Jeremiah had prophesied (Jeremiah 29:10)—with not only a return but also a restoration of the glory and majesty of the Davidic kingdom.

The reign of David was considered by all the high-water mark, politically and economically, for the nation of Israel. According to the prophetic writings of the law and the prophets, a son of David was destined to sit on the throne of a kingdom characterized by unprecedented fruitfulness, justice and righteousness (see Psalm 132:10–18).

Several years after the first group began rebuilding Jerusalem, Zerubbabel was installed as the new king. He was indeed a descendant of David. But in the following years, the nation of Israel never came close to regaining the glory and splendor evident during the reign of Zerubbabel's ancestors, nor of fulfilling the prophecies of the restored kingdom.

In the five centuries between the return from Babylon and the birth of Christ, Palestine served as a middle ground in the great tug of war between armies of the ancient world. Great nations from the East (the Medes, Persians, Assyrians) and from the West (Egypt, Greece, Rome) would alternatively rise up as the preeminent world power. And every time there was a change in the balance of power, the people of Israel wound up being dominated by the political and cultural force of another foreign nation. So their cultural captivity did not end when they went home to Jerusalem.

Can the Kingdom Come?

For five hundred years the Jews had been waiting for the Messiah, who would put an end to all this instability once and for all. A son of David would rise up, overthrow the invaders, sit on the throne of his father and fulfill the prophecies concerning the restoration of the kingdom. Periodically hopes would arise (as in the days of the Maccabbean revolt), only to be followed by disappointment. After many such disappointments, sects arose that followed the teaching of religious leaders known to us as apocalyptics. These were teachers who, after many failed messianic hopes, had given up on the restoration of the kingdom in history.

The phrase *this present evil age* came to represent the belief that the current world system was so dominated by Satan and his demons that it would be impossible for God's Kingdom to be established. Consequently the Kingdom would come only in the next age, or the "new age" (yes, pagan spiritualists have stolen the word) after God intervened with an apocalyptic event that would gain victory over the oppressors—that is, the "great and very terrible" day of the Lord (Joel 2:11).

The similarities between then and now are painfully obvious. Christians who have ascribed undefeatable powers to Satan have given up hope for the Kingdom of God to become a dominant cultural influence in present time. Hiding in their spiritual enclaves, they have nothing left to do but wait and hope for any form of victory to be accomplished by the Second Coming of Christ. They have fallen victim to a bankrupt eschatology.

Where Is the Messiah?

In many ways the late twentieth century fostered a spiritual climate similar to that of first-century Palestine. The fullness of time had come for the unveiling of the Messiah, and messianic pretenders were out in full force. Each attempted to gather followers who, with the help of God's supernatural, apocalyptic intervention, would drive out the Romans. Most of these counterfeit saviors met Israel's messianic expectations perfectly. Many were eventually arrested and executed, exposing their fraudulence to the world.

When Jesus the Christ arrived on the scene, the Jews were looking for a deliverer after the order of King David—a leader who would eliminate their external problems, liberate them from the power of Rome and set up an external Jewish kingdom. They were seeking political redemption and were eager for vengeance. They expected the Messiah to depose the half-Jewish Herod, ascend the throne of David and restore long-forgotten glory to Israel. This was their vision of the restoration of the Kingdom.

But instead of training revolutionaries and plotting the overthrow of Rome, Jesus was far more interested in the condition of men's hearts and how they lived their lives. Throughout the gospels His interest in the "inner" Kingdom outweighed His concern for political justice and national independence. Yet because the messianic paradigms were so deeply ingrained, the Jews tried to either crown or kill the Messiah who refused to become a puppet of either Rome or the Sanhedrin.

Probably one of the most amazing dimensions of revelation concerning the Kingdom of God and the Messiah comes to light in Peter's sermon on the Day of Pentecost. In fact, it is the key to interpreting all the Old Testament prophecies about restoring the Kingdom.

"Men and brethren, let me speak freely to you of the patriarch David, that he is both dead and buried, and his tomb is with us to this day. Therefore, being a prophet, and knowing that God had sworn with an oath to him that of the fruit of his body, according to the flesh, He would raise up the Christ [the Messiah] to sit on his throne, he, foreseeing this, spoke concerning the resurrection of the Christ, that His soul was not left in Hades, nor did His flesh see corruption. This Jesus God has raised up, of which we are all witnesses.

"Therefore being exalted to the right hand of God, and having received from the Father the promise of the Holy Spirit, He poured out this which you now see and hear. For David did not ascend into the heavens, but he says himself: 'The LORD said to my Lord, "Sit at My right hand, till I make Your enemies Your footstool."'

"Therefore let all the house of Israel know assuredly that God has made this Jesus, whom you crucified, both Lord and Christ."

Acts 2:29–36

Jesus was made both Lord *and* Christ—Ruler and Deliverer. This epiphany could not have come easily to Peter. It was the result of three years of careful observation culminating in personal revelation. The disciples themselves, Peter included, were predisposed to understand the prophecies in terms of an earthly throne. Even after the resurrection they were still asking, "Lord, when will You restore the Kingdom to Israel?" (see Acts 1:6). The content of Peter's first sermon, then, almost certainly originated in the post-resurrection teaching of Jesus, who for forty days spoke "of the things pertaining to the kingdom of God" (Acts 1:3).

Peter's sermon on the Day of Pentecost took five hundred years of Jewish prophetic interpretation and turned it on its head. Christ's resurrection and ascension to the right hand of the Father fulfilled the prophecies concerning the restoration of the Davidic throne. Consequently the Jewish believers had to rethink every other interpretation and expectation of the Kingdom. This was not an external Kingdom, yet it was one that would dominate the nations of the earth by the power of the Holy Spirit that had been poured out on them.

Peter went on to say that Jesus was the One they had been waiting for all this time. "You just crucified the Messiah," he boldly proclaimed. "Now He has been exalted to the throne of God as your Judge."

Since the return from Babylon, they had been waiting for their Messiah to come and establish God's divine justice by judging the wicked and exalting the righteous. Now the day of the Lord was on them and, in an ironic twist of fate, *they* had become the bad guys!

How did Peter's words affect those in the crowd? "When they heard this, they were cut to the heart, and said to Peter and the rest of the apostles, 'Men and brethren, what shall we do?'" (Acts 2:37).

A Kingdom Without Borders

The Jews had expected that all military power, political authority and cultural influence would be overthrown by the zeal of the Messiah. What they got instead was a tiny seed planted among all the nations, which were overgrown with all sorts of cultural and religious scrub brush. The seed of the Kingdom was destined to grow until it became a tree that was larger and more influential than all the other bushes of the field (see Matthew 13:31–32).

It is easy to see how zealots, radically committed to the restoration of national Israel, would have been disappointed with Jesus. They lacked the patience for such small beginnings or this internal-to-external strategy. Consequently they did not recognize their Messiah or the character of the Kingdom of God, nor did they understand how the prophecies of restoration would be fulfilled. They rejected Jesus and continued to look for a messiah in the leadership mode of King David. They were spiritually blind to the identity of the Messiah, the character of the Kingdom and the restoration of God's rule over all the nations.

The Kingdom of God, simply defined, is the rule and reign of Jesus Christ. That rule is expressed in the human heart before it is ever manifest in the human community. Jesus said, "My kingdom is not of this world. If My kingdom were *of* this world, My servants would fight. . . . My kingdom is not from here" (John 18:36, emphasis added). The word *of* reveals that the origin and source of life are not found in the carnal realm.

But we should not misunderstand this to mean that this realm is unaffected by Jesus' Kingdom. Nothing could be farther from the truth! The Kingdom is rooted in the sovereign rule of almighty God throughout eternity and is progressively revealed in the carnal realm. In fact, the prophet Micah declared that all the nations of the earth will eventually come under the influence of the Kingdom and the authority of the One who sits on the throne:

> It shall come to pass in the latter days that the mountain of the LORD's house shall be established on the top of the mountains, and shall be exalted above the hills; and peoples shall flow to it. Many nations shall come and say, "Come, and let us go up to the mountain of the LORD, to the house of the God of Jacob; He will teach us His ways, and we shall walk in His paths."
>
> Micah 4:1–2

The Kingdom of God encompasses every being—in the heavenly realm and on earth—who submits to His righteous rulership. The Kingdom, transcending the power and glory of any earthly realm, is not limited by time, space, geography, nationality or language. It is the most expansive government in all of history. It is utterly without borders. The authority of King Jesus progressively expands throughout human history as the Gospel is proclaimed and demonstrated.

Here is where *we* come into the picture. This mission will be fulfilled only through the ministry of men and women of destiny who, like Daniel, commit themselves to demonstrating the character of the Kingdom in a culturally relevant manner.

The famous Methodist missionary Dr. E. Stanley Jones revealed the strategy for transforming a generation:

> For the Church to be relevant the answer is simple: Discover the Kingdom, surrender to the Kingdom, make the Kingdom your life loyalty and your life program; then in everything and everywhere you will be relevant.[1]

Beyond the Beatitudes

The teachings of Jesus and the apostles emphasize that the aim of the Gospel is to produce internal change deep within the human heart. That transformation is progressive, continuing only as we bow our knees to the Lordship of Jesus and acknowledge His sovereign rule over our lives. The internal government of Jesus Christ produces righteousness, peace and joy in the Holy Ghost, not only in the human heart but also in the human community. This is what Jesus preached, and it set Him radically apart from the Mosaic economy.

The law of Moses said, for example, "Thou shalt not commit adultery" (Exodus 20:14, KJV). Jesus said, "Whoever looks at a woman to lust for her has already committed adultery with her in his heart" (Matthew 5:28). Obviously the ethics of the new covenant and of the Kingdom go far beyond legalism. What matters is not just what we *do* to live in and advance the Kingdom, but our attitude of the heart beyond all we do.

Some theologians minimize the importance of the Beatitudes because they contain no systematic theology. But those words of Jesus are more than just one of His many teachings. They are the very heart and soul of the Kingdom. Those principles of righteousness are the constitution of Christianity, revealing the moral standard by which we are to live our lives and interact with others:

> "Blessed *are* the poor in spirit, for theirs is the kingdom of heaven.
> "Blessed *are* those who mourn, for they shall be comforted.
> "Blessed *are* the meek, for they shall inherit the earth.
> "Blessed *are* those who hunger and thirst for righteousness, for they shall be filled.
> "Blessed *are* the merciful, for they shall obtain mercy.
> "Blessed *are* the pure in heart, for they shall see God.
> "Blessed *are* the peacemakers, for they shall be called sons of God.
> "Blessed *are* those who are persecuted for righteousness' sake, for theirs is the kingdom of heaven.
> "Blessed *are* you when they revile and persecute you, and say all kinds of evil against you falsely for My sake. Rejoice and be exceedingly glad, for great is your reward in heaven, for so they persecuted the prophets who were before you."
>
> Matthew 5:3–12, emphasis added

The Beatitudes describe the essential character of Kingdom citizens and reveal the ethical conduct required of true disciples of Jesus Christ. These revolutionary principles require the inner transformation of one's attitude toward eternal issues. They turn ordinary ideas upside-down and demand a response from us that is foreign to the lower nature of unregenerate man. These attitudes do not manifest themselves in our lives naturally; they originate in a supernatural realm.

Doing Them, Not Just Saying Them

Frankly, there is nothing attractive about these Beatitudes in and of themselves. They certainly do not appeal to the sinful nature of fallen man! In the same way that many did not recognize the King of kings when He arrived, the Kingdom of God is also often overlooked. It requires a radical shift in our thinking and expectations—one that comes neither easily nor naturally.

The English word *beatitude* comes from the Latin word *beatus,* meaning "perfect blessedness or happiness." Each of these nine principles begins with the Greek word *makarios,* which has been translated "blessed, fortunate, or to be envied."[2] Jesus is showing us that the one who follows these principles will be blessed of God and made to be envied by others. These principles, if followed, produce the results that provoke nations to jealousy.

We show the world how to live when we:

Manifest humility of life in the midst of arrogance and pride.

Live a lifestyle of repentance and intercession in the midst of denial and blame displacement.

Live with sensitivity and teachableness in the midst of selfishness.

Manifest genuine dependence on the grace of God in the midst of religious self-righteousness.

Manifest mercy and grace in the midst of anger and vengeance.

Manifest purity of soul in the midst of a deceitful culture.

Stand for truth, justice and peace in the midst of apathy and complacency.

Respond in love and graciousness when we are persecuted and ridiculed.

Stand unflinching in the face of popular opinion, esteeming Kingdom values above our acceptance by others.

Christian bookstores are filled with cards, plaques and posters advocating these Kingdom principles, yet our culture remains largely unchanged. Millions of Christians have settled for the *language* of the Kingdom without adopting its *practice*. Our only chance of reforming the culture comes when the ethics of the Kingdom become more than religious clichés. They must become the principles that govern all of our lives.

What society is looking for is the power of transformed lives. When the Church surrenders and really begins to live under the authority of King Jesus, she will, in the eyes of society, produce evidence that demands a verdict. When we fully demonstrate these Kingdom principles, we will show the world a quality of life that is available to them also.

Are You Ruled by the Constitution?

Why would anyone want to persecute people who are living the kind of life we have just described? The mystery lies deep in the innermost parts of an unregenerate man who, when confronted with the truth, refuses to forsake his wickedness. He is offended by the goodness of others—by their happiness and by their prosperity. He chooses deceit and injustice over purity and truth. He revels in selfishness and self-righteousness.

But regardless of whether such a person accepts or rejects you, Jesus says this is how He has designed life to be lived.

The Beatitudes deal with the reign of the Lord Jesus Christ in the deepest parts of our heart. The Kingdom is manifested from the inside out. It is as if Jesus were saying in the Beatitudes, "Once you have dealt with this inner issue of Lordship, then we can go public." Many Christians are frustrated in their efforts to work their way into a place of cultural dominion because they have not allowed Jesus' constitution of Christianity to rule their hearts and souls. Many people are not quite ready to sit in a place of social and cultural influence. They are still struggling with the issue of Lordship. Whose constitution will rule their lives?

God has promised to exalt those who have committed to seeking first the Kingdom and His righteousness (see Matthew 6:33). When we prove ourselves capable of discipling the nations, like Daniel and his companions, God will position us for cultural dominion.

I am convinced that the Holy Spirit is working with this generation on the *ethics* of the Kingdom, not just the *proclamation* of the Kingdom. You may have been saved for twenty years and believe everything in the Bible, including the sacred footnotes and the holy maps, but the real issue is, Have you ever been conformed to the ethics and constitution of the Kingdom? You may subscribe to the royal law of love, but are you *living* it? You may believe in purity and holiness, but are you demonstrating them? You may profess faithfulness to God, but are you sacrificially giving? You may believe in "not forsaking the assembling" of God's people, but are you committed to the corporate gatherings of the local church? It is one thing to accept His sacrifice, but another thing altogether to live under His rulership.

The new birth is not simply a ticket to heaven; it is a change of governments. Heaven is what it is not just because God created it to reveal unspeakable glory, but because Jesus Christ rules it from His throne. There He is not only celebrated as the Son of God, but He is obeyed as the King of kings. Our submission to His ultimate Lordship is the essential character of the Kingdom.

How Do We Establish the Kingdom?

When Jesus sent His followers into the world to disciple the nations, He clearly had global impact in mind (see Matthew 28:19–20; Mark 16:15). But establishing the Kingdom of God involves more than preaching the Gospel and rescuing the souls of men and women from eternal separation from God. Where do we begin the process of preserving and transforming our culture?

Ground zero is where we begin demonstrating the character of the Kingdom. Before we will ever influence the heart of a generation, we must first earn the right to be heard. This is why the lifestyle of believers is so important: People are watching us to see how we handle our resources and responsibilities. They connect our beliefs with our actions. "Let your light so shine before men," said Jesus, "that they may see your good works and glorify your

Father in heaven" (Matthew 5:16). When we live in a way that honors God, we become salt and light to an unbelieving world.

Another way we affect those around us is through participation in Christian organizations, such as local churches, parachurch ministries and world missions. If you minister in one of these ways, you have a priceless opportunity to demonstrate the effectiveness of the Kingdom when it is given preeminence among a group of people.

A third occasion for global impact is found in the opportunity to express the value system of the Kingdom in the midst of the systems of Babylon—that is, in science, the arts, media, industry, economics and public education. When Christians advance into every sphere of society, exemplifying the character of the Kingdom, we show the world that there is a better way of living. Success does not have to be traded in for integrity, humility and obedience, although many have been duped into believing that we must settle for one or the other—prosperity or generosity, success or humility, excellence or mercy. The Kingdom offers us the opportunity to succeed in life without following the same rules by which the Babylonians play.

Finally we have been given the opportunity for societal reformation through political lobbying and advocacy. Much of Daniel's career was spent in the inner chambers of the Babylonian government, where he served as chief adviser to King Nebuchadnezzar. Through the political arena, challenging as it is, each of us has been given the opportunity to influence the civil institutions that control society. This might mean an action as simple as voting or as complex as running for office or working to enact a particular piece of legislation. In Western democracies everyone has the privilege of participating in public policy decisions, and we should use the opportunity to honor the Lord and expand the character of the Kingdom.

Serving God by Influencing the State

What do scores of both Catholic and Protestant monarchs, along with the Emperor Constantine, Oliver Cromwell and some present-day Christian activists, have in common? They all gave in to the temptation to radically discredit or forcefully eliminate their political, cultural and religious opponents in order to establish a physical Christian empire.

In such a state, faith and righteousness are mandated by rule of law, and enforced with severe penalties. The character of this type of external, physical, religious Kingdom can be seen in the fundamentalist Islamic states that exist in Asia and the Middle East. Idealism has given way to intolerance, oppression and domination. The beauty of liberty has been crushed, and the voice of justice silenced.

Few Christians today have a vision for that form of government. But whenever we assume that righteousness is established in a culture by judicial legislation, then we are to some degree advocating the same outcome.

There is no greater area of controversy within the Church than over whether Christians should become involved in shaping the culture through the political process. There are those who believe, based on a misconception of the nature of the Kingdom, that we should abandon the culture. And, on the other hand, we have witnessed a resurgence of misguided fundamentalists who, in recent years, have attempted to restore the law of Moses in society.

Our hope does not lie in political redemption. It is not enough to enact laws that reflect the righteousness of God, if the rule of Christ has not been established in people's hearts.

Please don't misunderstand. We *do* need to pass righteous laws and elect moral leadership at every level of society. But we must continually remind ourselves, and those around us, that the Kingdom of God is established by Jesus' Lordship in the hearts of people. Laws against unrighteousness are only stopgap measures as we humble ourselves, pray and work for another spiritual awakening.

More than fifteen years after the Watergate scandal that undid several political careers, former presidential advisor Chuck Colson wrote, "Christians cannot afford to continue to confuse access to the Oval Office with political influence; nor can we put all of our hopes and energies in the political basket. Invitations to White House dinners don't assure political pull; nor can politics promise the penetrating societal changes we seek. In their high expectations of politics, many Christians also misjudge the source of true societal reform. In reality, it is impossible to effect genuine political reform without reforming individual and, eventually, national character."[3]

Think of the rise and fall of the great kingdoms of this world—the empires of Greece, Rome and Charlemagne. Consider the British Empire, the Bolshevik revolution and Nazi Germany. The kingdoms of this earthly realm, no matter how vast, well-organized or committed to their ideals, eventually fade into the history books. But after two thousand years, the Kingdom of God continues to expand. It is a Kingdom without end. The seeds of servant leadership planted in the heart of man by Jesus Christ will continue to grow until it overshadows every other tree in the field of history.

God has not called everyone to be involved in the political arena. As far as we know, Daniel—a remarkable leader who served faithfully in Babylon under the very kings who opposed his nation, oppressed his people and decimated his culture—was the only Jewish prophet to spend his entire ministry working as a public servant for a heathen empire. He successfully served three foreign kings and two pagan governments in a career that lasted seventy years.

Daniel demonstrated the character of the Kingdom even when he could easily have betrayed the Babylonians and brought them down. (During the seven years when Nebuchadnezzar was out of his mind, who do you suppose was running his kingdom?) This servant leader refused to compromise his integrity even when surrounded by rotten politicians, New Age charlatans and perverse pagans. The fact that Daniel maintained a lifelong reputation for unimpeachable integrity and unswerving commitment to the Lord makes him an important model for Christians in the twenty-first century.

Daniel and his Hebrew companions lived, as Jesus did, in the presence of sin, as servants to unrighteous men, without allowing the presence of sin to overwhelm them. In the end, the influence of the Kingdom won out. And if you are faithful and walk in the character of the Kingdom, it will for you, too.

8

RULING IN BABYLON

> If Christians are not relevant in the mundane, how
> are we going to be relevant in the profound?
>
> Pastor Erwin McManus[1]

I once heard an amusing anecdote about a man who jumped off a ten-story building. While the passersby screamed in horror, the man looked perfectly calm as he plummeted to his death. As he passed the window of a fifth-story apartment, he called to the terrified occupant, "Don't be afraid, everything's all right—so far!"

This apocryphal story reminds me of the attitude we Christians often display toward our current cultural crisis. In spite of the fact that we are rapidly plummeting toward destruction, we are happy and content that everything is still all right, so far. Our economy is relatively stable, so far. Our families are safely tucked into the supposed security of our suburban neighborhoods, so far. And we still have the privilege of quietly worshiping God on Sunday mornings behind the stain-glassed windows of our preferred church buildings, so far.

Our condition is not unlike the one Israel found herself in during the summer of 605 B.C.—the year she lost her independence and was made a vassal state by Babylon.

At that point in history, three nations were engaged in conflict for world domination. For three hundred years Assyria had ruled the world from the north Euphrates valley with Nineveh as its capital, but now she was growing weak. Babylon, located in the south Euphrates valley, was becoming increasingly powerful. And Egypt, which had ruled as a world power almost a thousand years before, was once again becoming ambitious.

Jeremiah was born into this political instability and called by God to lead his people in revival, restoration and reformation. Almost twenty years into his ministry, Babylon prevailed by breaking the stronghold of Assyria and crushing the power of Egypt in the battle of Carchemish. At that precise moment in history, Jeremiah was plunged into spiritual controversy, for at least three reasons.

First, he had spent twenty years prophesying that Babylon would be victorious over Judah if she did not repent and forsake her sin. Second, when there seemed to be no hope of Judah's repentance, Jeremiah urged her to submit to Babylon in order not to be destroyed. And finally, after counseling his countrymen to submit to their oppressors, he then prophesied that Judah would eventually recover, only to destroy Babylon and dominate the world.

After considering these unusual facts, we can see why God had to deliver Jeremiah from fear and insecurity when he was called into the prophetic ministry of destruction and reconstruction. The man was about as popular among the Babylonians as Rush Limbaugh would be at the Democratic National Convention!

The French have a saying: "The more things change, the more they stay the same." So we find ourselves today in a postmodern situation that resembles the one in which Jeremiah prophesied.

Have you ever noticed that most of the Bible was written while God's people were behind enemy lines? Significant portions of the Old Testament were played out while the Israelites were in bondage to Egypt, Assyria, Babylon or Medeo-Persia. The entire New Testament was lived out while Israel chafed under Roman occupation. The patriarchs and prophets clearly understood what it was like to be held captive by a hostile society.

During the first decade of Daniel's seventy years of exile, the remaining citizens of Judah carried on with business as usual. The Babylonian captives were all but forgotten by the majority of Israel. There were no recorded prayer vigils, no visits by hostage negotiators, no yellow ribbons tied to the trees. The captives were resigned to their fate. But all that changed when they received the prophetic message from Jeremiah.

The prophet was writing to people of God who had been taken captive by a hostile society. They were oppressed by a nation with little consideration for their faith in God. And Jeremiah's advice flew in the face of their past experience in captivity under the domination of the Egyptians and Assyrians. On the surface it seemed apparent that Jeremiah had formed an alliance with their captors. Rather than encourage them to revolt and break free from the bondage of Babylon, he was urging them to accept their confinement and settle in for another six decades!

Those who were suffering the hardship of life in exile did not, as you might imagine, receive this news with much enthusiasm. Apart from the obvious, why did Jeremiah try to placate them with his prophecy? Was this simply a ploy designed to lure them into a state of spiritual slumber? Or was God working in a way that was less than apparent?

The Seven Components of Reformation

After blues guitarist Eric Clapton released one of his best-selling singles, "Change the World," many social activists, identifying with the soulful lyrics, adopted this beautiful ballad as their own personal anthem. More than ever before, it seems, Christians and non-Christians alike have come to believe that global transformation is possible in our generation. But the haunting question remains: *How?*

Jeremiah 28–29 reveals seven components of biblical reformation in a nation. Originally written to the captives of Nebuchadnezzar, these principles are relevant to our own cultural crisis and serve to awaken the spiritual and social consciousness of any nation. Although the instructions are not all listed in biblical order, they are designed to work together in spiritual synergy.

1. We Must Acknowledge and Honor Spiritual Authority

These are the words of the letter that Jeremiah the prophet sent from Jerusalem to the remainder of the elders who were carried away captive—to the priests, the prophets, and all the people whom Nebuchadnezzar had carried away captive from Jerusalem to Babylon. (This happened after Jeconiah the king, the queen mother, the eunuchs, the princes of Judah and Jerusalem, the craftsmen, and the smiths had departed from Jerusalem.)

Jeremiah 29:1–2

Jeremiah's first step was to address those who sat at the gates of the city. Rather than subtly spread subversion and insurrection, the prophet appealed to those occupying the seat of authority in society. Jeremiah was acknowledging the principles of submission and authority. He understood that the anointing flows from the head down, and that if you turn the head, you turn the body. So he wrote to those capable of carrying out his prophetic instructions: the elders, priests, prophets, eunuchs, princes, craftsmen and smiths.

The same principle was at work throughout the three-and-a-half-year ministry of Jesus. Have you ever wondered why He spent so much time addressing the Pharisees of the day? Why didn't He just ignore them as He "went about doing good, and healing all that were oppressed by the devil" (Acts 10:38)? As startling as it may seem, He consistently focused His attention on them because of the role they played in the authority structure. The ecclesiastical organization of first-century Palestine had immense bearing on the political, social and cultural condition of the nation, so Jesus challenged the Pharisees—the spiritual gatekeepers of His day.

In Matthew 23:13 Jesus said, "Woe to you, teachers of the law and Pharisees, you hypocrites! You shut the kingdom of heaven in men's faces. You yourselves do not enter, nor will you let those enter who are trying to" (NIV). As spiritual gatekeepers, the scribes and Pharisees possessed the authority to open the door to revival, restoration and reformation—or to close it for the whole generation.

The same principle is found in Numbers 13–14, where the twelve spies returned from Canaan after investigating the land for forty days. Ten of the spies said, "We are not able to possess it. Even though the land is flowing with milk and honey, there are giants in the land." Only two spies, Joshua and Caleb, believed the Israelites were capable of defeating the enemy. Yet in spite of the faith of these two men, Israel was sentenced to forty years in the wilderness.

Have you ever researched the identity of the ten spies who brought back the evil report? The book of Numbers identifies them as the "heads of the children of Israel" (Numbers 13:3). They were the spiritual gatekeepers of their generation.

Once again, the prophet Joel enjoined the priests to "weep between the porch and the altar" (Joel 2:17). He knew that if you turn the head, you turn the body.

So Jeremiah interceded for the gatekeepers of his day. This is also the time for us to pray for the gatekeepers of *our* generation.

2. We Must Regain Historical Clarity

> Thus says the LORD of hosts, the God of Israel, to all who were carried away captive, whom I have caused to be carried away from Jerusalem to Babylon.
>
> Jeremiah 29:4

Anticipating Judah's propensity toward blame displacement, Jeremiah began his instructions by reminding her of the reason for her captivity. "Don't forget who orchestrated these events," he said. Jeremiah knew that by reminding the exiles of the One who had caused their captivity, he was reminding them of the reason for their captivity. This was his attempt to reconnect them with their history, in order to position them for their destiny.

Surrounded by a culture hostile to their faith, the captives could not afford to waste another day in the depths of despair. Nebuchadnezzar's court was not without an agenda. Their oppressors were not neutral in their disposition. Their plan was to reeducate and reposition the exiles, thereby repopulating the land, in effect, with the culture of Babylon.

We face the same agenda. To forget the past is to repeat it. If we want to see spiritual and social reformation in our nation, we need to be reminded of the character of the men and women who set sail in search of religious liberty; of the biblical foundations on which our nation was built; of the purpose behind its formation; of the biblical content found in our documents of freedom; of the price that was paid to ensure our freedom; even of the failures of our nation over the last two centuries.

To forget the past is to abort the future. As Christians we need to be reminded of our spiritual and theological foundations; of our creation, fall, redemption, restoration and destiny; of the principles of responsible submission to spiritual authority; of our biblical commission to reach the lost and disciple the nations.

There is power in the act of righteous remembering. Righteous remembrance is the act of reviewing the past in order to strengthen our character and avoid repeating the same mistakes. As twenty-first century Christians, we must remind ourselves that we are connected with something much bigger than us. God's purpose predates our personal perspective. This thing did not begin with us. We are joined with a great cloud of witnesses.

To see the Kingdom of God is to see the bigger picture. The Kingdom is that unbroken line of continuity that keeps us grounded to the past and the future. Jesus said the Kingdom "is like a householder who brings out of his treasure things new and old" (Matthew 13:52). To understand the Kingdom is to understand "ancient-future" faith. God's Kingdom has always existed, and it has been revealed progressively through every covenant God has instituted in time and eternity.

3. We Must Establish Economic Viability

Thus says the LORD of hosts . . . Build houses and dwell in them; plant gardens and eat their fruit.

Jeremiah 29:4–5

You can imagine the shock that must have registered in the hearts of these captives, on hearing Jeremiah's instructions. The prophet actually expected them to put down roots in this foreign land!

When writing about Jeremiah's prophetic charge to the citizens of Babylon, Bob Beckett differentiates between the perspectives of renter and owner. The owner landscapes the house, paints the siding, repairs the roof and puts up wallpaper; whereas generally a renter is unwilling to invest this kind of time, expense and energy. Why should he? The place does not belong to him. But Jeremiah is challenging the captives to avoid developing a renter's mentality.

Citing Jeremiah 29 Beckett, a pastor who has committed himself for life to his church and city, writes:

> Think about this passage in light of making your own territorial commitment. The children of Israel hardly considered Babylon their home. They longed for the day they could return to Jerusalem to get on with their lives. But God was telling them through the prophet Jeremiah to live their lives fully in the place where He had brought them. He was reminding them that He was the One who had put them there, and while they remained, they were to get on with the business of living life and blessing the land.[2]

One of the primary signs that we have overcome the transient mentality of hyper-dispensationalism (an expectation of the imminent return of Jesus Christ) is when we begin to build strong multi-generational businesses.

Robbed of a theological incentive to "plant vineyards," my spiritual forefathers did not plan for the future. To put down their roots very deep was, to them, a sign of disbelief in Jesus' very soon coming. Their tentative efforts to build businesses, therefore, were never very successful.

Listen, by contrast, to the admonition of Deuteronomy 8:18: "You shall remember the LORD your God, for it is He who gives you power to get wealth, that He may establish His covenant which He swore to your fathers, as it is this day." Our mission as the Church is to co-labor with Christ to bring forth the will of the Father in this present age. To "establish the covenant," then, is to reveal the promises of God to those who have neither seen nor heard them.

What is the key to establishing the covenant in our generation? To discover God's will concerning prosperity. If we cannot afford to take the message to the nations, we will never (in the words of Deuteronomy) establish the covenant in our generation. If we cannot afford television equipment and airtime; if we cannot afford to produce books and distribute literature; if we cannot afford a plane ticket and two weeks off work to feed the hungry and clothe the naked, then how will we establish the covenant in our generation?

It takes prosperity to build schools and establish universities to train nationals to reach their own nations. God's covenant provides for prosperity because it takes resources to establish the covenant in a generation. The man or woman who clings to poverty, ostensibly as the will of God, rejects the establishment of the covenant in his or her generation. Many times religious people view prosperity as selfish—and, indeed, it can be. But you can also be selfish in your poverty, because to hold onto poverty is to reject the establishment of the covenant in your generation.

When you find a genuine covenant man or woman—someone committed to fulfilling the purposes of God in his or her generation—you will find an individual who has settled the issue once and for all, who no longer struggles with whether or not prosperity is the will of God. This person has been delivered from the religious thinking that equates poverty with godliness, and he is seeking to be blessed—not to enrich himself and to make his life comfortable, but to acquire the resources necessary to bless others and reach them with the Gospel.

4. We Must Develop Family Stability

Jeremiah continued his prophetic instructions concerning the reformation of Babylon by encouraging the exiles:

> Take wives and beget sons and daughters; and take wives for your sons and give your daughters to husbands, so that they may bear sons and daughters—that you may be increased there, and not diminished.
>
> Jeremiah 29:6

Just think about the startling implications that are found here! The Jews were living as captives in a pagan culture, subjected to the oppression of foreign military rule. Their future seemed hopeless, their prospects tenuous. Yet Jeremiah said, "Even though you're captives in a strange land, one that doesn't embrace your value system, unpack your bags. Get married. Buy houses. Plant gardens. Raise children. And change your generation."

This advice is diametrically opposed to the fearful "family planning" advocates who warn us today, "This is the worst moment in history to bring innocent children into the world. How will you protect them? The world is an evil place just waiting to devour them. Why sacrifice unborn generations on the altar of selfish gratification?"

But Jeremiah, in spite of social upheaval, war, famine, crime and pestilence, realized that the enemy would be displaced only through the seed of the righteous. Essentially he was saying: "In spite of the fact that you may even have to send those children to a Babylonian public school, in a Babylonian district, in a Babylonian educational system, in a Babylonian city, in a Babylonian nation, which is ruled by Babylonian culture, go ahead and fill your quiver with bright, young, impressionable arrows!"

Jeremiah knew that, rather than contributing to the problem, those unborn generations were, in fact, the solution to the problem. With six decades of captivity remaining before them, those exiles had been prophetically positioned by God to reclaim the cultural landscape through multigenerational ministry.

Likewise, when we train our children in the ways of righteousness, and then send them out to exercise dominion in the earth, we are reclaiming the culture for Christ.

Multigenerational ministry, simply put, is understanding that the purpose of God usually takes at least three generations to implement. Furthermore, whatever He builds usually endures at least three generations. He is the God of Abraham, Isaac and Jacob. And the promise, as Peter preached at Pentecost, endures "to you and to your children, and to all who are afar off" (Acts 2:39).

The enemy has attempted to impede the progress of the Kingdom through generational disconnection. By alienating fathers from sons, and mothers from daughters, he has been able to destroy continuity among the generations. Thus, rather than building on the successes and failures of the previous generation, each generation is forced to start all over and relearn the lessons that should have been taught them by their parents. Righteous families provide the foundation for spiritual and social reformation in a nation.

In the past few years we have witnessed a trend in society toward home-based businesses. Sociologists call it "cocooning," a merger of the concepts of career and childcare. But this is nothing new. The strategy for world dominion has always flowed out of a home environment. God intended for Adam and Eve to rule the world from their home in the Garden. And Jesus Christ Himself, seated at the right hand of the Father, governs the universe, through the Holy Spirit, from His home in the New Jerusalem.

Let me say a word to mothers who have set aside their careers for the sake of raising families. Perhaps you feel as though you are prevented from making a difference in the community because you are focused on bottles, diapers and runny noses. Remember, the hand that rocks the cradle rules the world. Even in the midst of our captivity, God has given us the opportunity to transform the nation through the coming generation.

5. We Must Take Social Responsibility

Seek the peace of the city where I have caused you to be carried away captive, and pray to the Lord for it; for in its peace you will have peace.

Jeremiah 29:7

Follow me carefully through this scriptural paradox. As difficult as it is to face, the Lord says we find our peace in the peace of the city. That is not to say we cannot live in peace while the world around us struggles in confusion or conflict. We can. Our peace is not of human design; it is of spiritual origin. In fact, God has designed a lifestyle whereby we can live in health while the world is ravaged by incurable diseases, and raise our families in peace while society loses one more generation to despair and rebellion.

But even though our peace is not contingent on world conditions, it is connected to the peace of the city, in this regard: As a compassionate Christian, I grieve to see suffering in the lives of those around me. I am troubled to see the sick and diseased, even if I am walking in divine health. I am sad to see people living in poverty, even if I am blessed with the provision of heaven. I am disturbed to see the deterioration of our nation, even though my greater allegiance is to another Kingdom. And I must act on my compassion, since "faith without works is dead" (James 2:20).

In that respect, then, my peace is connected to the peace of the city. When the city is blessed, I have cause to rejoice with those around me who have also been blessed. My concerns are set at peace.

6. We Must Recover Spiritual Integrity

"The prophets who have been before me and before you of old prophesied against many countries and great kingdoms—of war and disaster and pestilence. As for the prophet who prophesies of peace, when the word of the prophet comes to pass, the prophet will be known as one whom the Lord has truly sent."

Jeremiah 28:8–9

Jeremiah was commissioned to prophesy during a spiritually tumultuous time. Not only were the people in despair of their captivity, but another prophet, Hananiah, had arisen to prophesy immediate deliverance, even though God did not intend to deliver them for seventy years. The people's desire for freedom was so great that even Jeremiah confirmed the words of this false prophet. It was only after he came to terms with the people's captivity that he was able to discover the heavenly strategy for victory.

I am convinced that Hananiah was motivated by a combination of frustration and compassion. He was frustrated at the captivity of his people and determined out of compassion to make their deliverance happen. But God had a different perspective. Because of their rebellion, He had actually caused them to be carried away into captivity. It was not an unmitigated attack of the devil on society; it was the law of sowing and reaping. Judah was subject to the very laws that she had set in motion through her disobedience and rebellion.

If we are to live as a prophetic people, we must be willing to say what God says, even when it goes against the tide of public opinion. And if we are to live as a prophetic people, we must be comfortable with silence when God is not speaking. Frankly, most of us are extremely uncomfortable with the silent years. But if you are uncomfortable with a sovereign silence, then you will yield to the pressure to speak on God's behalf, even when He is not speaking. You will find yourself motivated by human need and compassion, the desire to help a suffering person on God's behalf, rather than by the inspiration of the Holy Spirit.

If you want to see reformation in the nations, starting with your own, then you must rebuild the ruins of spiritual integrity.

In the wake of the premium our culture places on tolerance, we Christians are seldom held responsible for our actions. If anyone tries to hold us accountable, we simply change churches and repeat the process somewhere else. Consequently we spread unrighteousness from place to place. And since we seldom leave alone—rather, we leave with others—we litter the highway of holiness with broken lives and fragmented relationships. Instead of growing from glory to glory, we move from failure to failure, because we lack the divine order that comes only when we embrace the rule of the Kingdom.

Living in an age of self-rule has blinded many people to an understanding of the importance of divine order. What does this mean? To embrace divine order is to acknowledge that we are incapable of ruling our lives independent of the Supreme Ruler of the universe. We must allow King Jesus to structure our lives so that we live in harmony with the will of the Father. It is to surrender our lives to the government of heaven. Divine order is the result of our willingness to accept Jesus as both Savior and King. To perceive Jesus Christ as any less than the incontestable Ruler of our lives is to diminish His purposes—not only in our lives, but among humanity in general.

If we will see spiritual transformation in our communities and neighborhoods, we must be prepared to embrace the principles of divine order. The order of the Kingdom is inseparably interwoven with its opportunities. And when we forsake that order, our cities become a barren wasteland.

The prophet Isaiah, a contemporary of Jeremiah, revealed an important key to revival, restoration and reformation: "When Your judgments are in the earth, the inhabitants of the world will learn righteousness" (Isaiah 26:9). The world is still looking for a standard—people who walk what they talk, live what they preach and deliver what they promise.

As humiliating and painful as it was, Jeremiah led the way in rebuilding spiritual integrity.

7. We Must Rediscover Biblical Integrity

"Thus says the LORD of hosts, the God of Israel: 'I have put a yoke of iron on the neck of all these nations, that they may serve Nebuchadnezzar king of Babylon; and they shall serve him. I have given him the beasts of the field also.'" Then the prophet Jeremiah said to Hananiah the prophet, "Hear now, Hananiah, the LORD has not sent you, but you make this people trust in a lie."

Jeremiah 28:14–15

As we seek to tune our ears to the frequency of heaven, we must remind ourselves that the Scriptures take precedence over every spiritual gift given to the Church.

What does the Word of God say about the desire of heaven to change the earth? What is the attitude of the Father toward the reformation of the nations? Is God finished with the planet, or is He still drawing us into His eternal plan?

I believe that, along with a revival spirit, we need a theological and even an eschatological awakening. Let's listen intently for the scriptural summons that will break the back of situational eschatology and reveal the heart of God for the nations.

9

DISCOVERING YOUR PERSONAL MISSION FIELD

Our problem in evangelism is not a lack of training. The problem is that we don't love enough. Do
you need training to talk to your grandchildren?

Leonard Sweet

Just when you think you have it all together,
God does something to bring you down to reality. Several years
ago I set out on a missionary journey, arranged by the Holy Spirit,
that could not have been more religiously awkward. It cut so sharply
against the grain of every habit, experience and religious tradition
of mine that I felt like Peter sitting on the housetop in Joppa, per-
plexed at the leading of the Lord.

It was a simple plan: personally infiltrate popular culture; go to people where they are; enable the Gospel to become incarnate in a bizarre, ungodly culture; and become an honest but unconditional friend of sinners. In other words (and here is the radical concept), do what Jesus did!

Following this plan sincerely and effectively can be a challenge for any Christian. We have a lot of ideas and practices that tend to isolate us from the cultural mainstream and make us irrelevant to the average Joe. I had these obstacles to overcome, too—in fact, I had them in spades. To understand what an unlikely candidate I was for what can amount to cross-cultural outreach, consider some of the extreme elements of my background and religious heritage.

As the son of a pastor, I cannot remember a time when I did not want to preach. When asked at three years of age, "What do you want to be when you grow up?" I replied, "A preacher of the Gospel and a game warden!" I succeeded at the first goal. I distinctly remember hearing God calling me at age seven to serve my generation as a pastor.

As a fifth-generation minister, I was conducting my own revival meetings at age fifteen. Even as a teenager, I was naturally oriented toward public ministry. The pulpit was my turf, and I was confident and relaxed speaking to an audience of any size. (I felt, like most preachers, the bigger, the better!)

I spent the early years of my ministry building fences—between the Church and the world, between my church and other churches, between my denomination and other denominations, between the clergy and the laity. I built my fences rock-solid, constructing them with Scriptures taken out of context and biblical principles misapplied to support my personal views. When not building new fences, I found myself having to defend those I had already put up. It was an exhausting process, keeping the boundary lines clearly defined between the Church and the world, and the saints corralled within the lines!

Even though my denomination was pretty much ignored by the non-Christian community because of our faith and zeal, we considered ourselves the spiritual elite. We were proud to call ourselves dyed-in-the-wool premillennial dispensationalists and we expected the Church to be raptured at any moment. Since there was almost no time left on God's clock, trying to save a godless culture destined for destruction was, to us, like polishing brass on a sinking ship. Most of our denominational ministers boldly asserted that efforts to preserve or stir up righteousness in the culture would only delay the Lord's return, and consequently work against God's end-time purpose. So we made no efforts to save the ship, only (as the old hymn goes) to "rescue the perishing, care for the dying."

If you wanted to put a sociological label on us, we were not simply subcultural or even countercultural; we were anticultural. Having rejected almost every aspect of contemporary society, we were at war with the culture. As a child I had not been allowed to participate in or even attend public sporting events, watch television, go to the movies or listen to anything but Gospel music—the reason being, "You don't know what that might lead to." My boyhood church might as well have had a large sign over the pulpit declaring *No!*—because that was the answer to any question we children asked. So I became a dedicated isolationist, and proud of it.

But throughout public school I began to attempt to build personal relationships with my unsaved classmates, with limited success. Religious restrictions made it difficult for me to relate to them on any level deeper than casual friendship. My parents, as church-planters, were forced to reach out to the unsaved community, but their outreach was expressed primarily through knocking on doors and inviting people to attend our church services. Although my father preached about the transforming power of Christ in the human heart, the church took extraordinary safeguards to ensure that the culture would not overpower us. My frustration began to mount. How could I reach my unsaved schoolmates if I could scarcely communicate with them?

My tenure at Bible college only served to aggravate the problem. I will never forget the Monday afternoon when I sat in Homiletics 301 and listened to another young preacher deliver his first sermon, aptly titled "God Hates the Sinner." To my amazement, the professor applauded at the conclusion of the message.

My frustration came to a head in my first year of pastoring. Sleeplessness drove me out of bed in the middle of the night. I found myself lying prostrate on the floor, frustrated and heartsick.

Although I had perfected the craft of fence-building, I realized that I was harboring a secret longing to build bridges.

In one defining moment, I cried out, "God, I'm tired of building fences. Make me a bridge-builder!"

I told no one of that prayer. But the following month I handed in my denominational credentials and set out to discover the place where God was moving me.

Before long I found myself in the presence of Christians who, unlike me, appeared free from the trappings of religious legalism. Their selfless love and tireless giving helped free me from the spiritual bondage that had restricted the administration of grace in my life. I felt alive for the very first time. Each day was filled with new discoveries as I explored the depths of true righteousness, peace and joy in the Holy Spirit. Still, I seldom ventured beyond the four walls of our spiritual community into the great unknown.

Twelve years later, while I was pastoring, a man with a reputable prophetic ministry stood on the platform of my church and directed a message directly to me: "God has heard the cry of your heart and has chosen to make you a bridge. You will experience the discomfort of having people walk over your life in order to enter into their promised land, but the reward will be well worth the price you have to pay."

That message provided the confidence I needed to begin the process of penetrating the culture.

The Adventure Begins

Which brings us back to my missionary journey.

It began with a visit to the doctor's office. The preaching part of being a pastor was easy. It was all the other aspects of overseeing a fast-growing church that weighed heavily on my mind and were taking a toll.

"Terry, you've got to do something to relieve some of this stress," the doctor said. "If you don't find an outlet, the pressure is going to kill you. Have you thought about golf?"

"No. . . ."

"What about tennis?"

"I don't think so."

"Racquetball?"

Nothing the doctor suggested interested me. I could just see myself trying to relax during a five-hour game of golf while nothing was getting done back in the office. Did I really want to deal with additional anxiety over the time it was taking to alleviate the stress? The net result could be worse.

Almost as an afterthought, the doctor asked, "Was there anything you really liked to do when you were a kid?"

Church *was* what I did growing up. There were simply not many other options. The only other activity that fueled my fire, apart from ministry, was having a pack on my back, a hunting rifle under my arm and a night out under the stars.

"Well, that's it!" the doctor cried as if he had discovered the cure for cancer. "Have you ever hunted with a bow and arrow? I think you need to take up archery. It's a year-round sport."

Which is how I became a bow hunter.

Without arguing the merits of either hunting or bow-hunting, I will say simply that I dove into the sport wholeheartedly, and that it did indeed become a great stress-reliever. Whether competing in an archery tournament or sneaking up to within forty yards of a nine-hundred-pound brown bear in the remote Alaskan wilderness, this sport demands a degree of concentration unmatched by any other I have participated in. While I am in the field, archery requires my full attention, leaving me no room to worry about any of the challenges associated with pastoring a church and ministering to people. While hiding in the brush just thirty yards from an African lion, with nothing but a bow and arrow in your hands, nothing in the world can possibly distract you from your mission.

There is, however, another aspect of bow hunting that I had not anticipated: other bow hunters.

They are, by and large, a pretty rugged bunch. Most are far more comfortable with that solitary experience than they are with most social activities. Few I met at first were Christians, let alone Bible scholars. And I quickly discovered that I had ventured way out of my cultural enclave. When sitting around the fire in an African hunting camp or standing around a picture album in the local taxidermy shop, I found myself out on the edge of the conversation. My fellow hunters obviously needed ministry, and I could not help but feel that God was the One who had put me into those situations. But I had no idea how to relate.

The initial pressure I felt to share the Gospel with those guys was probably motivated more by religious obligation than by genuine concern. For a pastor with few non-Christian friends in his life, I was learning to relate the hard way—and discovering a lot in the process.

Arriving late one evening in a hunting camp on the Athabasca River in northern Canada, I walked over to the campfire and shook hands cordially with the other hunters before excusing myself and settling into my tent. It was almost impossible for me to find sleep that night as I dreamed about the next seven days of hunting and fishing.

Early the next morning I stumbled out of the tent and over to the campfire for a hearty breakfast. I was greeted by a group of silent, glaring hunters. Obviously something was wrong, but for the life of me, I could not figure out what had happened to transform this hunting party from the jovial group I had met the night before to the angry mob standing around the morning campfire.

The next six days were indescribable. When not scowling at me, the other hunters were either mocking televangelists or telling perverted jokes. I endured their hostility patiently, reminding myself that they did not know my vocation and that it must be coincidental. How could I be the target of their resentment if they did not know I was a preacher?

Nothing in the hunting camps I had visited previously compared to the depravity of these men. There were times when it took everything in me to hold my peace and remain friendly in the face of such antagonism. My tongue was raw from biting it as I attempted to demonstrate the love of Christ.

On the final day of the hunt, as I was packing my belongings and preparing to leave, the worst antagonist walked into my tent and sat down on my cot.

"Well," he said, "you passed the test."

"What test?"

"The preacher test."

"What in the world are you talking about?"

"Listen," he said, "we all know what you do for a living. When you walked up to the campfire the first night, I recognized you from a television program I saw when I was channel surfing a few nights earlier. You know, the program with the lady with the big hair and the fake eyelashes."

My blood ran cold.

"After you went to your tent, we decided to do everything we could to make your life miserable. We wanted to see if you were a fake. I expected you to get mad or religious on us, or avoid us altogether, but you didn't do any of those things. You passed the test.

"And by the way," he concluded, "I feel terrible about some of the things we said. I'm really sorry."

I sat there too stunned to speak. I remembered the times that I was within seconds of rebuking the whole lot of them. I had felt like calling down fire from heaven! I thought about how difficult it had been to stay engaged in conversation when I had wanted to retreat to my tent, to the safety of the religious zone. I was extremely happy that I had endured!

When we emerged from the tent, several other hunters filed by, one at a time, with sheepish looks on their faces.

"Sorry," they said. "You can hunt with us anytime."

Since that morning seven years ago, Mark and I have developed an unusual friendship, and I have had the opportunity several times to share the Gospel with him.

A Stunning Discovery

Let me tell you a secret about pastors, if you have not already figured this out. Most of us preach from the pulpit about things we are going through ourselves.

Having been made aware of my painful inability to relate to contemporary culture, I began to address the issue with my congregation. One Sunday morning, while preaching about lifestyle evangelism, I got an inspired whim.

"How many of you here this morning have five unsaved friends?" I asked the congregation. "Not just co-workers or acquaintances, but five unsaved people with whom you have a meaningful relationship? If you do, raise your hand."

I knew I was addressing a topic that had everyone's interest. With time and experience, pastors, like other public speakers, learn to read their audiences. Generally you can tell what is striking a chord. But in this congregation of more than four hundred people, not a single hand went up. Everyone was looking at me as if I had asked for a volunteer to come up and explain Einstein's theory of relativity.

After pausing a few moments, I figured they had not understood, or else I had been mistaken and they were not paying attention. I repeated my question. Still no response.

"How about three?" I asked.

Nothing.

"Two? How about one?"

As I stood before the congregation, the reality of our cultural retreat hit me like a ton of bricks. In this rapidly growing church, with dynamic worship and vibrant ministry, fewer than ten percent of the people in our congregation had a meaningful relationship with a non-Christian. I was forced to face the fact that most of our growth was from transfers, not conversions. Even those who had actually been saved had quickly exchanged their unsaved friends for new ones within the religious community.

I had been under the impression that my social irrelevance and cultural awkwardness were due to the fact that I was a preacher with a pretty extreme background. This stuff was much easier, I had assumed, for people who lived and worked in spiritual Babylon. I discovered, however, that as a church we had become a "sub-culturalized" group. It was as if we were held captive in a foreign land by a people to whom we did not know how to relate, who spoke a language we did not understand and whose values contradicted everything we believed.

The options (as I pointed out in an earlier chapter) are few in such a situation. We could retreat into isolation and hang on till the end, thus sealing our fate as an irrelevant subculture. (I knew all about that option.) Or we could allow ourselves to be absorbed into the "foreign" culture, and thus compromise the integrity of our identity, beliefs and values. Or we could infiltrate and infect the whole with what we had, like the leaven that leavens the whole lump.

The challenge to my church, and to me as one of its members, was to become culturally relevant infiltrators, with no questions or second thoughts about our identity in Christ, and who carried that confidence with us into the mainstream of postmodern culture.

Becoming a Friend of Sinners

According to Leonard Sweet, professor of evangelism at Drew University, the crisis facing evangelism is great. Among these are the following challenges:

> In a culture of Bible believing churches filled with people who don't read the Bible. . . .
> In a culture of soul-saving churches filled with people who never get personally involved in soul-saving. . . .
> In a culture where consumerism is the number one religion. . . .
> In a culture where Deepak Chopra, Oprah Winfrey, and Larry Dossey are more authoritative voices than Moses, Jesus, or even Mohammed. . . .[1]

World evangelism is the hallmark of authentic Christianity. In the past century alone, committed missionaries have covered the earth, presenting the Gospel to millions of people in urban and rural settings. Recognizing the urgent need for postmodern evangelism, the Roman Catholic Church has committed to the process of reexamining her previous patterns, in order to create new models for the twenty-first century:

> The Polish Pope John Paul II established the Pontifical Council for Culture in 1982 because of his conviction that "the destiny of the world" hinges upon "the Church's dialogue with the cultures of our time." Admitting the impossibility of contextless theology— "there is an organic and constitutive link existing between Christianity and culture"—Pope John Paul insisted "the synthesis between culture and faith is not just a demand of culture, but also of faith. A faith which does not become culture is a faith which has not been fully received, not thoroughly thought through, not fully lived out."[2]

The goal of discipleship is to become like the teacher. Perhaps one of the surest signs of a true disciple of Christ is that person's ability to submit to Him without compromise, while at the same time being a genuine friend of sinners. The term *friend of sinners* was used in reference to Jesus, as a compliment by the sinners and in condemnation by the Pharisees.

The calling of Matthew, also known as Levi, shows how Jesus related to those whom the religious community had shunned:

> Passing along, Jesus saw a man at his work collecting taxes. His name was Matthew. Jesus said, "Come along with me." Matthew stood up and followed him. Later when Jesus was eating supper at Matthew's house with his close followers, a lot of disreputable characters came and joined them. When the Pharisees saw him keeping this kind of company, they had a fit, and lit into Jesus' followers. "What kind of example is this from your Teacher, acting cozy with crooks and riffraff?"
>
> Matthew 9:9–10, THE MESSAGE

Having spent the majority of my life in the Christian community, I have been blessed by the example of many wonderful people over the years. But I have known only a handful who have displayed the ability to love the Lord without compromise while being a genuine friend of sinners. I greatly admire these people because I see in them the same characteristics I see in Jesus. Here are four.

1. Postmodern Soulwinners Refuse to Be Confined by Cultural Barriers

Matthew was a tax collector, the lowest of sinners in the minds of the Jews. Tax collectors were seen as betraying the entire nation by collaborating with the Romans, an occupying force in Judea. If Jesus had consulted a public relations expert about choosing His inner circle, He would have been told that Matthew was the least desirable of all possible candidates. Many would recommend, in fact, that it would be better to lead an incomplete ministry team than to take on Matthew. Yet Jesus did not simply approve Matthew's application; He sought him out.

It does not matter who you are, where you come from or what you have done. We are all equally bankrupt before God, and come to Christ only by grace through faith. Some people are less aware of their own need and have a harder time giving up their connection to the world. Not Matthew. He understood his great need and was willing to sell out completely. He made no effort to negotiate down the cost of discipleship, as we see in some others who wanted to be one of Jesus' followers. This tax collector got up and left his money table to follow Jesus. That is total commitment.

After traveling in more than fifty nations and ministering to people from hundreds of different ethnic cultures, I have discovered that the greatest barriers to evangelism are not theological or even philosophical, but cultural. The greatest soulwinners of history are those men and women who have refused to be intimidated by the social barriers erected by society.

There was a time in our own culture when most people tolerated the Gospel and were reasonably open to the biblical worldview. No more. Just as many fundamentalists have circled the wagons in an attempt to protect their religious interests, many postmoderns have barricaded their doors in order to preserve their own way of living. Recall that it is the non-Christian community, for the most part, and not the Christian community, calling for the separation of church and state. Knock on your neighbor's door with a handful of tracts, and you will quickly discover that a "cold call" can produce a cool reception.

The key to infiltrating the culture is to build strong personal friendships with those you are trying to reach.

I began developing a friendship with one of my neighbors. Because of a negative experience with Christians, his wounds were deep and his suspicions well-founded. We found we were worlds apart in beliefs, values and ideas about how life is to be lived. But somehow we found common ground. It took a long time of building trust, but my love for this man empowered me to endure as his friend until his hostility to the Gospel began to weaken. Finally he was able to open his heart to the Lord. Just one week before this writing he asked me to baptize him. It has taken nine years.

2. Postmodern Soulwinners Are Secure in Their Identification with Jesus Christ

Many Christians are afraid to develop meaningful relationships with non-Christians because they do not understand the security of their own personal relationship with Jesus Christ. They expect the unsaved to reject them for their faith, and as a result they act defensively. But once you experience the new birth and discover who God has created you to be, you lose your fear of rejection and reach out to those to whom you have been sent to minister.

Mark was a high school kid who, after a long struggle with the Holy Spirit, finally walked the aisle of the church and dedicated his life to Christ. The following Monday he began sitting by himself in the school lunchroom. His friends had no idea what was going on. Unfortunately Mark is like a lot of Christians. He assumed that his new commitment to Jesus would automatically cut him off from his old friends. He expected them to snub him.

I have come to discover that the *anticipation* of rejection is often more devastating than the actual *experience* of rejection. Many times we never reach out to the unsaved around us because of our fear of rebuff. In fact, we anticipate it without giving others the benefit of the doubt.

There is an old story about a man who decided it was time for a promotion and salary increase on his job. He bolstered his courage, scheduled an appointment with his boss and began to prepare his argument. Anticipating refusal, he built his case like a trial attorney in a capital case defending the life of an innocent man.

When I walk into his office, the worker thought, *I will look him straight in the eye and demand my raise. And when he turns me down, I will say, "I've poured my life into building this company for twenty years." And when he refuses to accept my proposal, I will say to him, "Either you give me a raise or I quit!" And when he stares defiantly at me, I will storm out of the office and never return.*

After considering what he was up against, the man simply boxed up his personal belongings and left the office without even going to speak with his boss! His anticipation of a turn-down had left him paralyzed with fear.

Many times our attempts to reach our non-Christian friends leave us drenched in sweat while our knees are having fellowship with one another! In other words, it can be terrifying. When you realize that the one you are hoping to reach does not share your convictions, understand what you hope to accomplish, or, in some cases, embrace your values, it can be intimidating, to say the least. But Matthew was so excited about following Jesus that he threw a big party and invited all his sinner friends to come and meet Him.

Often people respond to you according to your expectations. If you anticipate rejection because of your association with Jesus, you will probably get it. If you are insecure or ashamed of who you are as a Christian, you will probably not attract a lot of converts.

Those who are genuine disciples and genuine friends of sinners at the same time do not hide who they are; they go in with the flag flying high. Theirs is not an in-your-face approach, but they are excited about Jesus, proud of their relationship with Him, and they talk about Him in an open and comfortable way. Perhaps Matthew was naïve enough to think that everyone would want to hear about Jesus. Effective infiltrators are able to maintain this spiritual innocence. Even though they may have been rejected at times, they do not let those experiences injure their faith, causing them to retreat into isolation.

3. Postmodern Soulwinners Are Unashamed in Their Love for Others

Jesus arrived on the scene at a time when Judea was being held captive politically by Rome and culturally by the influence of the Greeks. The Pharisees were the religious conservatives and fundamentalists of the day who tried to barricade Judaism against the intrusion of Greek culture. They prided themselves on their strict adherence to the Mishna—the traditions of the elders, the extra-biblical code of conduct that had developed over hundreds of years, going all the way back to the Babylonian captivity. For these leaders, zeal for the Law and traditions were more important than common-sense compassion—a point Jesus made in His parable of the good Samaritan. The Pharisees majored in sacrifice but flunked compassion. In fact, many of them wound up hating sinners.

This is not as uncommon as we might think. A former campus pastor recently described to me the events surrounding the summer he and his family spent living in an apartment complex surrounded by college students. Overhearing conversations among students that mocked Christians and Christianity made him think, *If they knew I was a dedicated believer, they probably wouldn't have anything to do with me.*

As the summer went by, there were several irritating incidents—cars blocking the drive, beer cans left around the pool, noise after hours. During one late-night party, the pastor went out to some of the students sitting around the pool and, with a tension he knew was discernible in his voice, asked them to please keep it down. One young man replied, "Sure, man. Sorry."

Returning to his apartment, he felt like the old ogre who used to live in the neighborhood where he grew up. *God,* he prayed, *why did I get upset with those guys? I love them and want to win them to Christ.*

Instantly there came the still, small voice of the Holy Spirit. *No, the truth is you hate them.*

His immediate reaction was to pray something like this: "O Lord, Thou knoweth that I loveth them!" But the Holy Spirit had put him in that situation for the express purpose of teaching him a life lesson.

You're right, Lord, he admitted. *I do hate them.*

Being bitter at people who reject you or what you stand for is a natural response. Even though the students had never made comments to him personally, nor had they shown him any unkindness because of his faith, this campus pastor had come to resent them—not for any actual rejection, but simply because of *anticipated* rejection.

"It was a painful encounter," he told me later, "one that really revealed what was in my heart. It made me see how much we need to be filled with God's love, not just our own human love."

Many Christians are the same way; we are just not so quick to admit it. We have developed an adversarial approach to evangelism and hold deep resentment against sinners—either for what they have done or said, or simply for what we imagine they might. It is the natural reaction of an isolationist group with a persecuted mentality. Many Christians are exactly like the woman I knew who invited her hairdresser to church, then blamed him for stalking her when he actually showed up! How different from Matthew, who simply assumed everyone wanted to meet his Lord.

We cannot relate successfully to an unevangelized, anti-Christian culture by following a simple formula. Some try to relate to people by purely external means. But wearing the latest designer clothing will not communicate the Gospel to secular people. There is nothing more embarrassing than seeing a fifty-year-old pastor with a toupee, pot belly and diamond stud in his ear attempting to be "relatable." Speaking the language and knowing the customs of contemporary culture are indeed like building a bridge. But if you are without the love of Christ, you have nothing to drive across that bridge that people want.

Reaching out to people to score a religious brownie point, or because we feel it is our religious duty, always comes off as disingenuous. Paul commented that a great sacrifice, a generous gift or a dynamic message without love is like a noisy gong and tinkling cymbal. Pure love, by contrast, is a transcendent language that crosses every barrier—even barricades of generation, culture and language.

4. Postmodern Soulwinners Practice the Ministry of Reconciliation

The opening scene of the movie *The Mission* reveals one of the more powerful moments in recent motion picture history. A Jesuit missionary sent to reach an isolated tribe in South America had been crucified by the very people he was trying to reach. Imitating the crucifix that hung on a chain around his neck, they tied his body to a cross and sent it washing down over a huge waterfall. Soon afterward his body washed up on the bank of the river where his companions were camped. Wasting no time in grieving, they buried the body of their slain companion and sent another member of the Jesuit order to minister to the tribe.

The only way to reach them, however, was to climb straight up the craggy face of the waterfall over which the murdered priest had just come crashing down. After hours of relentless climbing, the second priest barely managed to reach the top, where he entered the jungle. Knowing the tribe's love of music, he reached into his water-soaked pouch, pulled out a reed flute and began to play. Risking his very life, this missionary entered their world.

This is the kind of incarnational evangelism required to reach our postmodern world. After you watch *The Mission,* you will find your neighbors looking less intimidating than they did before!

Seeing the vital connection between his new identity as a son of God and his mission to reach his generation, Paul the apostle wrote:

> If anyone is in Christ, he is a new creation; old things have passed away; behold, all things have become new. Now all things are of God, who has reconciled us to Himself through Jesus Christ, and has given us the ministry of reconciliation, that is, that God was in Christ reconciling the world unto Himself, not imputing their trespasses to them, and has committed to us the word of reconciliation. Therefore, we are ambassadors for Christ, as though God were pleading through us: we implore you on Christ's behalf, be reconciled to God.
>
> 2 Corinthians 5:17–20

Two words in this passage reveal the key to our involvement in the ministry of reconciliation, and these words are given in an intentional order. First, the Greek for "ministry" is the word *diakonia,* from which we derive the word *deacon.* It is better defined as "a servant or attendant." Next, the Greek word *logos,* translated "word," literally means "the divine expression" or "the spoken word, including the thought."

Paul says that following the *diakonia* of reconciliation, we have been given the *logos* of reconciliation. In other words, we are the servants of reconciliation before we are the announcers of reconciliation. Only when we truly serve hurting humanity as instruments of reconciliation are we qualified to communicate the message of reconciliation.

Floyd McClung, a missionary leader who raised his family in the red light district of Amsterdam, once defined the challenge like this: "People don't care how much we know until they know how much we care." What is more important to you, to *serve* or to *teach?* Your answer to this question will reveal whether you want to simply instruct people, or actually reach them.

You cannot reconcile what you have not served. The very nature of the word *reconciliation* denotes personal involvement, a life commitment. *To reconcile* is to bring together opposing forces. This is what lifestyle evangelism is all about. "Christians and non-Christians have something in common," declares Rebecca Pippert. "We're both uptight about evangelism."[3] Reconciliation evangelism is predicated on the investment of one's life into a world that is foreign to us.

The nature of reconciliation requires personal contact, an investment of one's life into the life of another. This is the understanding of reconciliation that drove Jesus into contact with the broken, hurting outcasts of society. The ministry of reconciliation required that He be robed in the frailty of humanity. The prophet Isaiah foretold this: "He had no beauty or majesty to attract us to him, nothing in his appearance that we should desire him. . . . [He] was numbered with the transgressors. For he bore the sin of many, and made intercession for the transgressors" (Isaiah 53:2, 12, NIV).

When a president or prime minister sends an ambassador to a foreign land, the representative bears the seal of his country, which identifies him as one who represents the interests of that country's leader and who intercedes on his behalf. The Son of God, by contrast, did not bear the glory of His own position or authority, but humbled Himself to the lowest degree in order to identify with those He was coming to save.

Nor could He reconcile particular men and women to the Father by sitting on an elevated throne in heaven, detached from the affairs of humanity. He had to make contact with the thief on the cross in order to redeem him. He had to talk with the woman at the well in order to restore her to God.

Consider the position of a hostage negotiator. Before he can buy back the hostage's freedom, he has to place himself in a position that may not be comfortable. He may even have to step into a place of personal risk or grave danger. But to win the hostage's release, he will place himself in an environment not altogether friendly with his belief system. Doesn't that sound exactly like what Jesus did when He talked with the woman at the well? "Don't You realize that You're a Jew," she was asking, in effect, "and I'm a Samaritan, and this environment is hostile to You?"

When Jesus walked the seashores of Galilee healing the brokenhearted and setting the captives free, He was identifying with the broken and the outcast, while not sharing the experiences that led them into their state of brokenness in the first place. He did not relate to them on the lowest common denominator; He related to them on the basis of love.

How Much Do You Love?

Concerning my relationship with those in the world, my goals are to interact with others comfortably, to share Christ with them naturally and to love them unconditionally. These are not easy objectives—and, as a cross-cultural missionary to my own culture, I consider it all but impossible without a great deal of God's divine grace and love. But I have found that if you simply learn to love people, a lot of the other stuff works itself out.

Last Thanksgiving Day my wife ran out of some necessary ingredient early in the morning, so I was commissioned to go to the grocery store. After racing down the aisle, I hurried to the checkout line just in time to overhear the cashier telling a young woman impatiently that her food stamps were expired and that she could not buy the Similac baby formula.

The young mom, who appeared to be in her early twenties, rummaged through her purse and pulled out a couple of rumpled dollars. It was obviously not enough for the milk. The cashier just stood there, snapping her gum and looking disgusted. Finally the young mother apologized, closed her purse and turned to leave.

Then the Holy Spirit spoke to me. *Pay for the milk for her baby.*

I quickly moved forward, groping for my wallet. "Excuse me, miss, I'm supposed to buy that for you."

She said, "You're what?"

I took a deep breath. "I'm supposed to buy that milk for you. God bless you. Now have a happy Thanksgiving."

As the young woman walked away, the cashier sneered, "Well, that was a nice thing to do, but she probably had a valid coupon at home."

"Maybe she did," I countered, "but let me tell you something. I've never forgotten where I came from, and except for the grace of God, I would be right where that young lady is today."

For a moment the cashier stopped popping her gum. "I guess you're right, sir," she said.

I would like to be able to tell you that I led them both to Christ, right there in checkout lane number five in Albertson's grocery store. But I did have two minutes to sow a seed, and I did. Someone else will eventually reap the harvest.

Select the Right Bait

I have discovered that effective evangelism is not a one-size-fits-all proposition. No one evangelistic style succeeds for every person, everywhere, on every occasion. What works for one may not work for another.

Please don't misunderstand my point. I am not suggesting that the Gospel should be changed or modified to fit every individual we encounter, because the Good News is indeed a one-size-fits-all message. But we must tailor our evangelistic strategies, our ways of communicating our faith, to each individual. You cannot use one type of bait to catch every fish in the ocean. Whether you use a net, worm, lure or fly, fish can be caught in a variety of ways. But in order to connect with a specific fish, you have to use a particular kind of bait.

Once, while I was fishing in northern Canada with three other fishermen, we caught almost five hundred fish in one week. Unlike fishing for men, this was "catch-and-release" fishing. And those incredible northern pike were only hitting on a spinner lure painted like a five of diamonds playing card! They would not respond to any other lure. We tried every shape, size, color, smell and texture, but the fish responded to only one specific lure. Need I say that by the end of the week, that five of diamonds lure was battered, bent and stripped of most of its paint?

In like manner, we will reach our non-Christian friends only by discovering their interests, bearing their burdens and living authentic Christian lives before them. People respond to the message of the Gospel when it connects with a need in their lives. To be successful in reaching them, we must tailor the Good News to each individual. For an anti-fishing vegetarian, an invitation to a fish-fry evangelism dinner is not appropriate. A grandmother may not be interested to hear a professional athlete share the Gospel in a radical setting. We will genuinely connect with people only when we become sensitive toward their personal worldview and culture preferences. If we are going to offend people, let it be for the sake of the Gospel, not our cultural ineptitude!

There are numerous ways to reach out to the community. Among these are:

- Home Bible studies
- Birthday clubs
- Book reading clubs
- Mother's day off programs
- Medical missions
- Musical concerts
- Drama productions
- Activities for retirees
- Cultural awareness events
- Church-sponsored parks
- Church athletic programs
- Big brother/sister programs
- Benevolence ministries
- Voter registration
- Vocational training classes
- Career counseling
- Ecological awareness events
- Church-sponsored seminars on money management, debt reduction, investing, retirement, raising healthy children, building strong marriages, etc.

Regardless of the bait being used, we will succeed in reaching unbelievers when we identify with them spiritually. This will place us uncomfortably close to people who do not yet have a relationship with Christ, but we must not allow radical differences to prevent us from connecting with them in their alienation and pain.

Doing evangelism from a distance—leaving tracts in public restrooms, for example, or witnessing by e-mail—may feel better to us, because when we get close to people who do not know Christ, we can get hurt. And if we build relationships with people in our communities, they will eventually see us for who we are—either Christlike or hypocritical. This is risky and complicated and demanding. But the reward of seeing redeemed lives is well worth the risk.

10

L^EARNiNG T^O SPE^AK B^ABYL^ONI^AN

If I cannot imagine the apostle Paul as a pugna-
cious guest on *Nightline,* or citing a character's
anguished struggles with Roman Catholicism on
Homicide, then my apostle Paul—and my sense of
the Christian's cultural mandate—is too small.

Douglas Leblanc[1]

Come with me on an imaginary journey through
a typical non-Christian suburban household. Richard and Susan
Wilson are characteristic of their generation. As early baby boomers,
they were raised in an age when trust was as common as apple pie
and baseball. A daily diet of *The Mickey Mouse Club* provided lessons in life, morality and self-respect. They studied hard, esteemed
authority figures and believed in the American dream. Their out-
look on life was shaped by Sunday school attendance and participation in social clubs. Life was good and the future was bright.

But all that changed about the time the Beatles were singing, "You say you want a revolution. . . ." The shock waves of the 1960s are still being felt four decades later. What do you get when you combine social upheaval, violent riots, a controversial war, evolution, atheism, drugs and promiscuous sex? You get disillusionment, hopelessness and rebellion. The seeds sown in the lives of millions of baby boomers have continued to reap a devastating harvest long after the day the music died. We have sown to the wind and are reaping the whirlwind.

As we take our imaginary walk through the Wilsons' home one evening, it is impossible to ignore the difference that a few decades make. There is Richard sitting on the couch in the den, remote control in one hand and cold beer in the other. The movie he is watching on the Playboy Channel is enough to make his mother blush. Oblivious to everything around him, he stares at the screen as the pornographic images barely register beneath his stress. Richard's career is stalled and he is terrified about the future. Worried about whether he will be able to pay the mortgage three months from now, he has fallen into deep despair.

Susan is in the bedroom preparing to go out with her girlfriends for the third night this week. Her life is empty. She finds Richard callous and indifferent to her personal needs. Her therapist has encouraged her to leave him in order to find her soul mate. Her New Age guru keeps her focused on the spiritual aspects of life, but it does not seem to be working anymore. Her closest friend has recently suggested that she contact the psychic hotline in search of answers. She has contemplated having an affair, just to bring back the spark of living.

Suddenly the doorbell rings. After shouting at Susan to answer it and getting no response, Richard hauls himself off the couch and stomps to the door. When he opens it, he is surprised to encounter two young men who say they are visiting from the church around the corner. Seeing fun in intimidating a couple of Bible-thumpers, Richard invites them into the den to make their pitch.

Carefully positioning themselves so they cannot see the television, one of the young evangelists clears his throat nervously and launches into his pitch.

"Thank you for inviting us into your home," he begins. "We're here to invite you to our upcoming revival meetings. God is moving in a mighty way in our church. We are seeing the fire fall every time we have a service. It all began when we decided to go into our prayer closets to pray and seek the face of God so that He would heal our land."

Two minutes later, the staccato narrative ends and the young man falls silent.

Richard sits on the couch dumbfounded. What in the world is this guy talking about? A litany of questions flashes through his mind, erasing the weariness he felt moments earlier. Where did God move to? Why did the kid say the church burned down? What does God's face look like? How do you heal land?

Richard waits in that uncomfortable moment for someone to say something that makes sense, but the two young men have clearly finished their pitch. It is as if the one used up his entire vocabulary in one nervous burst of energy.

His desire to intimidate them forgotten, Richard tries to change the subject. "Isn't this weather great?"

"Yes," comes the one-word answer.

Another pause. "What about those St. Louis Rams?"

No answer.

Suddenly Richard wishes he could ask them the hard questions about life, family, eternity and Christianity, but he knows it would be a waste of time. He hauls himself to his feet and shows them to the door.

Then, after watching the timid missionaries retreat down the sidewalk, he resumes his seat in front of the movie, questions cast aside. *When will those spiritual dinosaurs ever learn to relate to the modern world?* he thinks.

Listener Empathy

Let's face it. Gospel tracts are not the best way to interact with an unsaved friend or neighbor. Drive-by shoutings and Gospel muggings will never transform the city of man or those who live there. In fact, Gospel bombardment can even be counterproductive. Far from incarnating the Good News or helping Christians identify with people in the world, it perpetuates an us-versus-them state of mind. Because of the isolation of the Church and our inability to relate, Christians resort to talking *at* unbelievers rather than talking *with* them.

While sitting in a Mexican restaurant eating dinner with my wife, I could not help but overhear a woman at the adjacent table preaching fervently to one of the waitresses. Every time this religious zealot spotted the hapless young lady scurrying by with plates or a tray of beverages, she would call out another Bible verse. To make matters worse, the staff knew very little English apart from the items on the menu.

For a while I was almost embarrassed to be a Christian. What bothered me most was not the message but the manner in which it was presented. As the woman's voice got louder and louder, the conversation became less and less private. You could sense everyone's growing contempt for the Christian and pity for the waitress. But the woman was so excited about her opportunity and about what she was saying that she was unaware of the atmosphere of growing hostility.

One of the symptoms of being a religious isolationist is that you have lost much of the ability to communicate naturally. Not only is your speech filled with religious jargon that is bewildering to non-Christians, but you lose your empathy as a listener. Christians can witness to non-Christians and think they are communicating effectively, not realizing how strange or even offensive their words are sounding. We have become far more comfortable in preaching *at* sinners, using the language of Jerusalem, rather than ministering *to* them in the language of Babylon.

And the truth is, in many ministry situations we would prefer for people to be quiet so we can deliver our message without interruption. While sharing the Gospel, I have actually had the following thought cross my mind: *Would you mind just being quiet so I can preach?* Usually there are several reasons Christians like me feel this way.

One is that if the person you are witnessing to responds with comments or questions, this can sidetrack the conversation, which is especially frustrating when you have a well-rehearsed presentation. Another is that this person might ask some difficult questions. If you are not secure in talking about your faith, sincere, open dialogue can be threatening. But propaganda and indoctrination are all about monologue rather than dialogue, and that would surely evoke the frown of Socrates, who advocated reasoning with one another in an honest and sincere search for the truth.

Another reason we talk at people rather than with them is that we assume they have little or nothing of value to say on the subject. But if you think non-Christians do not quickly pick up on that attitude, your "listener-empathy sensors" are in need of adjustment! The people all around you—your neighbors, your co-workers, the checker at the store, the young man at the gym—are looking for someone to affirm them, to listen to what they have to say, to love them, to show them a way out of their pain. And in order to do that, you must understand where they are coming from and learn to speak their language. As one Japanese evangelist stated, "We have twice as many ears as we do mouths, so we should spend twice as much time listening as we do talking."

The most outstanding characteristic of the ministry of Jesus, other than His miracles, was His ability to communicate effectively with common people, using language and illustrations they could understand. The Pharisees spent much of their time arguing among themselves on the finer points of theology, using words and concepts that had meaning only within their little world. One group believed that people should stand when reciting the *Shema* ("Hear, O Israel, the Lord our God is one Lord"), while the other group was convinced they needed to be sitting down. Common people could not have cared less.

Jesus is God incarnate, who came to our world and identified with us. His ability to communicate and identify with the masses—people just like us—was a dramatic contrast with the religious leaders. They were out of touch and so filled with jealousy over how Jesus connected with regular folks that they plotted to have Him crucified.

Evangelizing Across the Cultural Divide

Daniel and his friends received a three-year crash course in the language and literature of Babylon. "As for these four young men,

God gave them knowledge and skill in all literature and wisdom" (Daniel 1:17). At the end of the training period, they graduated at the very top of their class.

God brought the young Hebrews to the king's court as a witness for Himself. But the full impact of His glory demonstrated through them did not come until many years later. These guys spent a good portion of their lives learning the culture, language and history of Babylon, and then establishing their own credibility in the eyes of their peers.

I am not suggesting that we lie low as undercover Christians until we reach the pinnacles of power and influence. A *witness* is not something we do, it is who we are, and we cannot turn that off. But we can learn a lot from foreign missionaries about reaching people for Christ in our office buildings or talking to other parents after meetings at school. Trying to plant the Gospel in a foreign land without respect to the language, culture and history is presumptuous. Bridging the gap between evangelical Christianity and the reigning cultural status quo is not unlike the challenge missionaries face when taking the Gospel to an unreached people group.

Unfortunately, many Christian missionary efforts throughout history have been thinly veiled efforts at colonialization. Those who considered themselves more advanced attempted to impose not only their faith but also their culture, customs and worldview on the "poor savages" they had come to save. In certain denominations, evangelism was judged successful only if the converts assumed the trappings of Western civilization and brought their personal lives into conformity with Western dress, concepts of time and values of capitalism and democracy. Some missionaries went to great lengths to make tribal peoples worship in square buildings with steeples, read the Bible in English, sing English hymns and even wear suits and ties.

In such cases the true objective of cross-cultural evangelism was left unmet, due to a lack of understanding of the purpose of world evangelization. Rather then present the message and Person of Jesus Christ in the language and culture of the people, certain missionaries tried to convert them to Western culture as a sign that they had been genuinely born again.

Developing a New Language

There are a number of practical ways we can learn from misguided missionary efforts of the past and learn to communicate effectively with postmodern Babylonians. I have listed just a few ways in order to stimulate this process.

1. Observe Your Neighbors and Co-Workers

There is a world of inexpensive, highly interactive personal knowledge to be gained simply by observing those who live, work and play near you. Rather than succumb to the pressure to demonstrate your brilliant Christian leadership skills, quietly watch the way they interact (or not) with one another. Listen for telltale references to the factors that are shaping their lives, including sports, politics and entertainment. What television programs do they schedule around? Which movies are they fascinated with? Which entertainers are affecting their worldview? What philosophy governs their behavior? Based on your observations, learn to build relationships with these who live close to you.

2. Eat at New Restaurants Outside Your Normal Preferences

In the past decade, as I have been privileged to travel extensively overseas, I have observed new cultures and interacted with people who would not ordinarily intersect with my quiet suburban neighborhood. I have had equally meaningful exchanges, however, interacting with people in ethnic restaurants within my community.

Find and visit the local hangouts for teens, college students and special interest groups within your city. Warning: In order to learn anything, you must leave your judgmentalism at home or, better yet, bury it once and for all! Remember, you are there to learn how to connect, for the sake of reaching them (and others with the same values) with the Gospel.

3. Turn Off PBS and Watch Diverse Television Programming

An immense part of pop culture is framed by the entertainment industry. As postmodern reformers we must reclaim the positive elements in this powerful medium. Generation X is moved by the visual even more than the auditory, so check out what is showing on MTV and VH1. We must also seek practical ways to incorporate the power of the visual in our worship services, Bible studies and missions ministries.

4. Spend the Afternoon at Barnes & Noble Reading Everything in the Magazine Section

Almost twenty years ago a wise old preacher walked me through a bookstore and pointed out some titles of best-selling novels. When I politely inquired what we were doing, he responded, "Look at these titles. Can your sermon titles begin to compare with this level of creativity?"

That was a great starting point—and not the final destination. A sermon title alone is not enough to hold the attention of any group, let alone the MTV generation. Most effective television programs and music videos now seem to have three or four themes running simultaneously, with the picture shifting constantly from one story line to another.

Books, magazines, newspapers, periodicals, even comics provide us with an instant read on different aspects of postmodern culture. Take advantage of this information to form a strategy for counteracting the deception with biblical principles.

5. Go on a Journey of the Internet

If you have done much surfing of the Net, you have already been fascinated, and perhaps a little overwhelmed, at the sensory overload of cyberspace. But if you have done little of this, log onto the Internet and take a trip beyond your usual sites and boundaries. Or, if you lack the computer wherewithal, ask a web surfer to take you along for the ride. In the hands of a skilled navigator, you will see in an eye-opening way what men and women and young people today are focusing on.

An Apostolic Prototype

The apostle Paul is the premier example of cross-cultural evangelism. His effectiveness was demonstrated throughout all of Asia Minor. One of the clearest examples of the skill with which he crossed cultural barriers was his interaction with the philosophers on Mars Hill.

The apostle was in Athens waiting for his traveling companions, who had stayed in Berea to strengthen the new believers there. As was his custom, Paul reasoned with the Jewish and Gentile seekers in the synagogue. But he was never one to confine himself to a small corner of the community. He knew the Gospel was for everyone, both Jew and Greek. So before long he was a regular at the open-air market, which was not only a place to buy and sell, but also the communications nerve center of the city.

It was there, at the marketplace in Athens, that certain Epicurean and Stoic philosophers heard Paul preaching a new doctrine about the resurrection from the dead. At their invitation, the apostle went with them to Mars Hill, a small hill near the Acropolis where a council of Athenian leaders, known as the Areopagus, met to discuss matters of truth and wisdom.

With much of their day devoted to talking about philosophy, you can imagine how anyone with something new to say was welcomed by these learned men. They asked to hear from their visitor concerning this new teaching.

> Then Paul stood in the midst of the Areopagus and said, "Men of Athens, I perceive that in all things you are very religious; for as I was passing through and considering the objects of your worship, I even found an altar with this inscription: TO THE UNKNOWN GOD. Therefore, the One whom you worship without knowing, Him I proclaim to you: God, who made the world and everything in it, since He is Lord of heaven and earth, does not dwell in temples made with hands. Nor is He worshiped with men's hands, as though He needed anything, since He gives to all life, breath, and all things.
>
> "And He has made from one blood every nation of men to dwell on all the face of the earth, and has determined their preappointed times, and the boundaries of their habitation, so that they should

seek the Lord, in the hope that they might grope for Him and find Him, though He is not far from each one of us; for in Him we live and move and have our being, as also some of your own poets have said, 'For we also are His offspring.'"

Acts 17:22–28

When Paul, a master at cross-cultural communication, was around Jews, he spoke as an expert in the law of Moses and traditions of the elders. When in the presence of the Greeks, he quoted their poets and communicated as one of their own philosophers. What he said of himself was true: "I have become all things to all men, that I might by all means save some" (1 Corinthians 9:22). Paul became a servant to everyone in order to win anyone. As Joe Aldrich writes, "Evangelistic effectiveness is directly related to the ability to *become,* the ability to understand and relate to differences."[2]

Paul did not compromise his spiritual values for the sake of cultural relevance (as we will see in the rest of his address later in this chapter). Like Paul, postmodern missionaries have to understand which concepts are culturally adaptable and which are fixed. With essential concepts like blood atonement for sin, there can be no alteration—even though, once again, there *can* be more effective and less effective ways to communicate.

Relaying concepts cross-culturally can become very complex. Every culture across the face of the globe, for instance, has its own name for God. What a missionary has to determine is whether or not a particular word has so many non-Christian ideas attached to it that using it is less effective—or downright counterproductive. If so, he or she will have to find another word.

You and I have to communicate across cultural barriers in our own society, conveying concepts with terminology to which non-Christians can relate, but which is not loaded down with non-biblical implications.

Again, however, how we do this is not as important as who we are. Joe Aldrich continues, "The issue at stake is not what I need to *know* as much as what I need to *become.* The critical question is not, 'What *information* do I need to master?' as much as, 'What *identity* do I need to assume?'"[3] As I pointed out in a previous chapter, mistaken identity always results in wrong behavior. When we are seen as outsiders, then the other person reacts with suspicion and hostility. Sensing rejection, we typically respond one of two ways: We react defensively or we withdraw.

Instead let's learn from Paul, who, according to Aldrich, exemplified three principles of cultural sensitivity:

- Paul had a flexible conscience when it came to matters without moral significance.
- Paul was approachable because of his sensitivity to others' interests, concerns, circumstances, opinions and backgrounds.
- Paul's entire life was a lesson in self-denial and servanthood.

In Paul's remarkable encounter on Mars Hill, we can find timeless principles for communicating the Gospel across cultural barriers. Cultures come and go, but principles for relating cross-culturally remain effective in every generation.

Discovering Common Ground

This is why new converts can be the best soulwinners of all, more effective than professional evangelists with award-winning smiles or pastors with seminary degrees. New believers are not so far removed from the customs and language of the mission field on which they were saved. Even though the pages of their Bibles are still stuck together, new converts can relate to the rest of the "natives." They know where the unsaved and unchurched hang out, what they think and how they feel about professional Christians. They also know the arguments against the Christian faith. (Tragically, in their quest to discover the practical application of personal sanctification, they lose touch with the world whence they came and for whom Christ died.)

Discovering common ground requires more than simply running through the familiar list of socially acceptable questions: "What's your name? Where are you from? What do you do for a living?" We need to find common interests. Our quest may start with discussing a recent movie or best-selling novel. It may bring up concern over an international political issue or simply making ends meet. Find the common ground, then be patient.

Through a series of remarkable events in 1995, I was invited to a small gathering of pioneer Christian leaders in Great Britain to spend the afternoon with Queen Anne of Romania. My hosts were in the process of building a relationship with Her Majesty based on their involvement in the restoration of Romania following the Communist takeover of 1947.

Following a reception, we gathered around the queen, at her request, to pray for her beloved country. For the first few moments of prayer, I was far more conscious of the need to follow proper protocol than I was of this unprecedented opportunity to minister to an Eastern European sovereign. Suddenly the presence of King Jesus filled the room and Her Majesty began to experience her first encounter with the manifest power of the Holy Spirit. I watched with amazement as the centuries of royal custom began to bow to the spiritual hunger that was being awakened within her heart.

When it came time for us to return to the airport, she invited me, to my amazement, to ride with her.

"There's certainly no need for anyone else to take you to the airport," she said. "I am going, too. You will be my guest." And with that we were off.

My nerves were just a bit frazzled by now. After all, it is one thing to hold your own when surrounded by other guests who were also conscious of the dictates of royal protocol. It is something quite different to be riding alone in the back of a limousine with a queen. The ride to the airport, where Queen Anne would be meeting a private charter, took two hours. I expected it to take forever! But by the time we finally arrived, I was surprisingly comfortable in her presence.

What did we talk about during the ride? Well, when Queen Anne confessed to being a hunter, my fears instantly vanished. We had found our common ground. So on the way to the airport we discussed my two favorite subjects—wildlife conservation and the Gospel of Jesus Christ.

After finding the thinnest thread of commonality, many are tempted to charge into a confrontation about the other person's relationship with God. But if you do, you are communicating that you really did not care that much about the previous conversation. All you wanted to do was get an opportunity to proselytize.

Which poses a good question. Let me ask it as a reminder: Do you indeed care about your neighbor or co-worker as a person, or do you primarily care about preaching to him or her? Jesus related to people and was well received by them—not because He had a well-rehearsed sales pitch, but because He really loved them for who they were, right where they were.

By "discovering common ground," I also mean the common ground rules of meaningful dialogue and debate. When Paul spoke to religious Jews, he spoke as a Jewish rabbi. When his audience was Roman, he identified with them as a Roman citizen. To the Greek philosophers on Mars Hill in Athens, he framed his address in the format of deductive logic. Paul began with what was commonly accepted, and progressed logically, step-by-step, to Jesus Christ who rose from the dead.

Preaching an expository sermon from the law and prophets to an audience of Greek philosophers would have been as inappropriate as showing up drunk to speak at an AA meeting. I have overheard Christians in intense debates with nonbelievers, proclaiming in a deep, authoritative tone of voice, "The *Bible* says. . . ." But quoting Scripture verses and expounding on them presupposes an argument from authority. It is another way of saying, "The Bible says it, I believe it and that settles it." The problem is, most people living in Athens or Babylon—or Charlotte, for that matter—do not accept the Scripture as the final authority for their lives. So quoting a Bible verse to prove something (as opposed to quoting Scripture judiciously, as led by the Holy Spirit, to stir hunger in the other person) settles nothing. If your friend does not accept your source as the final authority, make your point another way.

The two most important things you must do in communicating cross-culturally is *speak the other person's language,* in order to relate to him or her, and *understand his epistemology,* or how he arrives at truth. If you miss on either of these points, you lose credibility.

Using the Power of Shared Beliefs

Your ultimate intention is to reveal the truth that is yet unknown to this person. To do that, you are well advised to start out by confirming what he or she already believes to be true. If you start out by saying (or implying) that every aspect of his belief system is simply wrong, while every aspect of yours is unquestionably true, there is a good possibility you will run into some resistance.

It is important to remember that all truth is God's truth, even if it is not religious truth. The law of gravity is true, even though it is not very "religious." In the same way, all truth is true, even if it comes from a questionable source. The "genetic fallacy" is the logical inconsistency that rejects a proposition simply because of its origin.

"That can't be true," says the evangelist, "because it comes from Hinduism." But suppose it is this proposition: *It is more blessed to give than to receive.* Well, yes, that *is* true. It may be surrounded by error, and it may not be the whole truth in a certain situation, but the proposition in and of itself is true. In such a case, confirm truth, but do it carefully. It is mentally easier to assert that the entire Bible is true while everything that a non-Christian thinks is wrong—mentally easier, but not very effective.

Paul began his address to the Athenians by referring to a time in their history when God revealed Himself to them. The following story is recorded in the writings of a third-century Greek historian, Diogenes Laertius.

In the sixth century before Christ, only a few years before the Jews were carried off to Babylon, Athens was smitten with a great plague. The leaders, after doing all they could think of to appease the gods, sent for Epimenides, a philosopher from Crete. Epimenides' prescription was based on three assumptions: first, that there must be an unseen god whom they did not know; second, that this god was great and good enough to stop the plague; and third, that this god would have mercy on them if they acknowledged their ignorance.

With those assumptions in mind, Epimenides instructed them the next morning to bring to him sheep that had not been fed, along with a group of stonemasons. The philosopher then ordered that the sheep, both black and white, be released and allowed to graze.

He prayed aloud to God, acknowledging their ignorance and asking Him to reveal His willingness, by means of a sign, to help them. The sign would be that either the black sheep or the white sheep would lie down while the others grazed.

It seemed foolhardy since all the sheep were hungry and anxious to graze. Nevertheless, it happened just as the philosopher had suggested. While all the black sheep continued to graze, all the white sheep lay down. So each white sheep was sacrificed on a stone altar that was built where the animal had lain down. The plague spread no farther, and within a week the citizens who were sick recovered. The Athenians built a statue of Epimenides and placed it in front of one of their temples.

Over the next few centuries, many of the stone altars had deteriorated or been torn down. But there was at least one altar still standing when the apostle Paul came to town. And it still bore the inscription *Agnosto Theo,* "To the Unknown God."

Because Paul knew the language, history and culture of Greece, he was able to begin his address at the Areopagus by establishing common ground: "As I was passing through and considering the objects of your worship, I even found an altar with this inscription: TO THE UNKNOWN GOD" (Acts 17:23). He was intentionally referring to a point in their history when God had revealed Himself to them. Paul also quoted a line from one of their own poets: "For we are also His offspring" (verse 28). Who do you suppose Paul was quoting? It is a line from a poem by none other than Epimenides.

If you want to reach a post-Christian generation, you have to build a bridge to where they are. You might begin by confirming a truth found in a contemporary song, movie, novel or news report. Once you have established rapport with them, you will be able to build a bridge to Jesus Christ.

This is not necessarily easy—but it is always effective.

The Journey to Babylon and Back

After you have built a bridge to another person's world, and after you have confirmed his or her concerns, bring everything back to

Christ and His Kingdom. Listen to the balance of Paul's address on Mars Hill:

> "Therefore, since we are the offspring of God, we ought not to think that the Divine Nature is like gold or silver or stone, something shaped by art and man's devising. Truly, these times of ignorance God overlooked, but now commands all men everywhere to repent, because He has appointed a day on which He will judge the world in righteousness by the Man whom He has ordained. He has given assurance of this to all by raising Him from the dead."
>
> And when they heard of the resurrection of the dead, some mocked, while others said, "We will hear you again on this matter."
>
> Acts 17:29–32

Paul himself wrote that the Gospel was a stumblingblock to the Jews, with all their false expectations about the Messiah, and that it was foolishness to the Greeks, who sought for wisdom (see 1 Corinthians 1:23). Some Greeks—the Gnostics, they were called—had attempted to synthesize the Gospel with Greek philosophy in order not to be so offensive to the Greek mindset. Not Paul. He had arrived at the point in his address to the Athenians where there was no way to avoid the nonnegotiable elements of the Gospel. Many rejected him at this point, but some became believers, including Dionysius. Tradition from the Church fathers has it that Dionysius became the elder of the church in Athens.

Paul is a prime example of someone who could reach across a great divide and influence a culture. He knew the language, he understood culture and epistemology, he was aware of critical common beliefs, and he was able to discern the elements of the Gospel that were flexible, according to culture, and essential doctrines that were unchangeable.

Most people of foreign cultures are honored when they meet a person who has taken the time to learn their language and customs. Usually they are eager to talk. For Daniel and his friends it was a matter of survival. For us it is a matter of choice and obedience to the Great Commission. Figuratively speaking, learning the language of Babylon is not as complicated as it seems. Over time our ability to talk with nonbelievers in a natural way may be more a reflection of our respect and consideration than it is of the complexities of their language and culture. Not only do we need to love people with the love of Christ, but we have to show them courtesy, even when they have wrong ideas, even when they are in bondage to sin, even when they persecute us. We cannot afford to become so passionate about being right that we forget to be kind.

As the earthly representatives of the Kingdom of God in this world, why would we not seek to express the presence, character and power of the King in every area of life? How did Jesus respond when confronted with these very issues in His generation? He reached out to Samaritans, Gentiles, children, harlots, tax collectors, legalistic Pharisees, insane demoniacs, rich young rulers, untouchable lepers, Roman centurions and fishermen. He ministered in synagogues, on the hillside, in the Temple, at weddings, in home groups and before the chief representative of Rome. Then He sent His own representatives out to every tribe, tongue, people group and nation.

From what area of life did He exclude Himself? When Jesus looked at the world, what aspect of Jewish or Roman culture did He consider to be outside the realm of His Lordship and apart from those things that are to be put under His feet?

Infiltrating the world is not so much a task we strike out on our own to do for the Lord, as if, for a disciple, it were an extracurricular activity. No, it is something we do simply by following the Master. Have you noticed that He is constantly headed in that direction? It is part of the very nature and character of Jesus Christ.

Learning the language of Babylon is like building an expansion bridge to connect with a very different world. Making contact is only the first step. In order to touch a person's heart, you have to communicate eternal truth with love and compassion. More importantly, to be like Christ is to identify with and be numbered among the transgressors, yet without sin. That was the challenge to Daniel in Babylon, to Jesus in Judea, to Terry Crist in a postmodern community—and to you, wherever you live.

Will you accept the challenge?

NOTES

Chapter 1

1. Allan Bloom, *The Closing of the American Mind* (New York: Simon & Schuster, 1987), p. 197.

2. *Eerdmans' Handbook to Christianity in America* (Grand Rapids: Eerdmans, 1983), p. 321.

3. Cited in Gene Edward Veith Jr., *Postmodern Times: A Christian Guide to Contemporary Thought and Culture* (Wheaton, Ill.: Crossway, 1994), pp. 44–46.

4. James C. Dobson and Gary L. Bauer, *Children at Risk: The Battle for the Hearts and Minds of Our Kids* (Dallas: Word, 1990), p. 19.

5. Leonard Sweet, *Sweet's Soul Café*, Vol. 3, No. 5–6 (n.p.: 1998).

Chapter 2

1. As quoted in "Seeking Christian Interiority: An Interview with Louis Dupré," *Christian Century* (July 16, 1997), p. 654.

2. *Christianity Today,* March 26, 1976, p. 27.

3. Terry Crist, *The Image Maker* (Lake Mary, Fla.: Creation House, 2000), p. 57.

4. Charles Colson, *How Now Shall We Live?* (Wheaton, Ill.: Tyndale, 1999), p. xii.

5. Bob Briner, *Roaring Lambs* (Grand Rapids: Zondervan, 1993), p. 70.

6. Howard F. Vos, *Archaeology in Bible Lands* (Chicago: Moody Press, 1977), p. 147.

7. Avraham Negen, *Archeological Encyclopedia of the Holy Land* (Englewood, N.J.: SBS Publishing, 1980), pp. 43–44.

8. Ray Bakke, *A Theology as Big as the City* (Downers Grove, Ill.: 1997), p. 87.

Chapter 3

1. Winkie Pratney, *The Daniel Files*, taken from the Internet.

2. Charles Sherlock, *The Doctrine of Humanity* (Downers Grove, Ill.: InterVarsity, 1996), p. 130.

3. Ray Sutton, *That You May Prosper* (Tyler, Tex.: Institute for Christian Economics, 1987), p. 125.

4. Bloom, *Closing,* p. 197.

5. Ibid., p. 204.

6. Cited in Herbert Schlossberg, *Idols for Destruction* (Wheaton, Ill.: Crossway, 1993), p. xviii.

7. All citations from H. Richard Niebuhr are taken from *Christ and Culture* (New York: Harper, 1951).

8. E. Stanley Jones, *The Unshakable Kingdom and the Unchanging Person* (Nashville: Abingdon, 1972), p. 19.

9. Carl F. H. Henry, *God, Revelation and Authority,* six volumes (Waco, Tex.: Word, 1976), Vol. 1, p. 13.

10. Matthew Henry, *Matthew Henry's Commentary on the Whole Bible* (Peabody, Mass.: Hendrickson, 1991), p. 1776.

11. Quoted in *The Forerunner* campus newspaper (Maranatha Ministries, 1988).

Chapter 4

1. Samuel Huntington, "The Clash of Civilizations," *Journal of Foreign Affairs* (summer 1993), p. 22.

2. David A. Noebel, *Understanding the Times* (Eugene, Ore.: Harvest House, 1991), p. 8.

3. J. I. Packer, as quoted in *Leadership Journal,* winter 1997, Vol. XVII, No. 1, p. 52.

4. David F. Wells, *God in the Wasteland: The Reality of Truth in a World of Fading Dreams* (Grand Rapids: Eerdmans, 1994), p. 48.

5. Edward H. Rain, quoted in *Understanding the Times* (Eugene, Ore.: Harvest House, 1991), p. 30.

6. James Orr, *The Christian View of God and the World* (Edinburgh: Andrew Elliot, 1897), p. 20.

7. Arthur Koestler, *The Act of Creation* (New York: Dell, 1964), p. 50.

Chapter 5

1. Francis Schaeffer, *A Christian Manifesto* (Westchester, Ill.: Crossway, 1981), p. 17.

2. H. Burtness, "Bonhoeffer, Dietrich," in *Baker's Dictionary of Christian Ethics*, Carl F. H. Henry, ed. (Grand Rapids: Baker, 1973), p. 67.

3. A. W. Tozer, *The Dwelling Place of God* (Harrisburg, Pa.: Christian Publications, 1966), p. 53.

4. Richard Lovelace, *The Dynamics of Spiritual Life* (Downers Grove, Ill.: InterVarsity, 1997), p. 279.

5. Ralph Wood, *A Commentary on Daniel* (Grand Rapids: Zondervan, 1973), p. 47.

Chapter 6

1. *The Atlanta Journal-Constitution,* Thursday, August 24, 1989. *The DeKalb News,* Sunday edition, August 9, 1989.

2. Earl Paulk, *One Blood* (Shippensburg, Pa.: Destiny-Image, 1996), p. 105.

3. William Temple, *Christianity and the Social Order* (London: SCM Press, 1950), p. 47.

4. Bakke, *Theology,* p. 34.

5. Paul Tillich, *The Irrelevance and Relevance of the Christian Message* (Cleveland: Pilgrim's Press, 1996), p. 13.

6. Ibid.

7. Abraham Kuyper, *A Centennial Reader,* ed. James D. Bratt (Grand Rapids: Eerdmans, 1998), p. 461.

8. Abraham Kuyper, *Lectures On Calvinism* (Grand Rapids: Eerdmans, 1931, 1975), pp. 9–30.

9. John Pollock, *Wilberforce* (Herts and Belleville, Mich: Lion, 1977), pp. 37–39.

10. George Gallup, Jr., *Forecast 2000* (New York: Morrow, 1984), pp. 113–123.

11. Bakke, *Theology,* p. 35.

12. C. S. Lewis, *Taliessin through Logres* (Cambridge: Cambridge University, 1948), p. 350.

13. Ibid., pp. 350–351.

Chapter 7

1. Jones, *Unshakable,* p. 19.

2. *Vine's Complete Expository Dictionary of Biblical Words* (Nashville: Thomas Nelson, 1985), s.v. "blessed."

3. Charles Colson, *Against the Night* (Ann Arbor, Mich.: Vine, 1989), p. 118.

Chapter 8

1. As quoted in Leonard Sweet, *Soul Salsa* (Grand Rapids: Zondervan, 2000), p. 82.

2. Bob Beckett, *Commitment to Conquer* (Grand Rapids: Chosen Books, 1997), p. 65.

Chapter 9

1. Leonard Sweet, *Postmodern Pilgrims* (Nashville: Broadman and Holman, 2000), p. xxii.

2. Leonard Sweet, *Aqua Church* (Loveland, Colo.: Group, 1999), p. 71.

3. Rebecca Pippert, *Out of the Saltshaker and into the World* (Downers Grove, Ill.: InterVarsity, 1999), p. 15.

Chapter 10

1. Douglas L. Leblanc, "Two Cheers for TV," *Books & Culture* (July/August 1998), p. 12.

2. Joe Aldrich, *Lifestyle Evangelism* (Sisters, Ore.: Multnomah, 1993), p. 66.

3. Ibid.

INDEX

Terry M. Crist has other books, video and audio products available. To obtain a catalog or to request more information about his church, ministry or apostolic network, please contact:

Terry M. Crist
SpiritBuilder Seminars
P.O. Box 8339
Scottsdale, AZ 85252

(480) 661-9209

Or visit his web site at www.terrycrist.com

Pastor Terry M. Crist is a leader whose influence has spanned the globe. In addition to serving as senior pastor of CitiChurch International in Scottsdale, Arizona, he has traveled extensively in more than fifty nations speaking in local churches, leadership conferences and on university campuses. The power of the Holy Spirit in his life, combined with his iconoclastic humor and sharp theological insight, makes the Word of God come alive in his teaching.

Terry Crist serves as the apostolic team leader of CitiNet International, a network of churches joined in covenant relationship for the purpose of advancing God's Kingdom. He is also the president and CEO of SpiritBuilder® Seminars and Resources.

The driving force in Terry's life is his desire to participate in the development of a glorious Church, a great global harvest and the dynamic establishment of the Kingdom of God in the twenty-first century. He has advanced this mission through writing nine books, and has appeared on various radio and television programs throughout the U.S.